CELIBATE PASSION

Published in San Francisco by Harper & Row, Publishers

1817 *New York, Hagerstown, San Francisco, London*

CELIBATE PASSION

Janie Gustafson

Grateful acknowledgment is made to the following to reprint sections from copyrighted material:

Harcourt Brace Jovanovich, Inc., for T. S. Eliot, "Little Gidding," *Four Quartets,* copyright 1943.

Macmillan Publishing Co., Inc., for Rabindranath Tagore, *Songs of Kabir,* copyright 1915; and for Rabindranath Tagore, *Fireflies,* copyright 1928.

The New American Library, Inc., for Lao Tzu, "Poems 6, 42, 64, 78, 76," *The Way of Life,* copyright 1955.

Paulist Press, for John of the Cross, *Ascent of Mount Carmel,* copyright 1958; *Dark Night,* copyright 1959; *Living Flame of Love,* copyright 1962; *Spiritual Canticle,* copyright 1961.

Random House, Inc., Alfred A. Knopf, Inc., for Kahlil Gibran, *The Prophet,* copyright 1951.

The Viking Press, for D. H. Lawrence, "The Phoenix," from *The Complete Poems of D. H. Lawrence,* copyright 1964, 1971 by Angelo Ravagli and C. M. Weckley.

All Scriptural quotations, unless otherwise cited, are taken from *The Jerusalem Bible,* ed. Alexander Jones (Garden City: Doubleday & Co., 1966).

My special thanks to Michael Leach, John Loudon, and Terry Sweeney for their expertise in editing this manuscript.

BV
4509.5
.G86
1978

Library of Congress Cataloging in Publication Data

Gustafson, Janie.
CELIBATE PASSION

    1. Christian life—1960–   2. Celibacy.
I. Title.
BV4509.5.G86 1978   248'.4   77–20439
ISBN 0–06–063536–3

78 79 80 81 82 10 9 8 7 6 5 4 3 2

To Terry, Theresa, and Patricia, who, by their love for me and their burning for God, are thrusting me ever deeper into the mysteries of celibate passion.

CONTENTS

PREFACE

THIS book has been four years in writing and twenty-five years in living. When I first put my pen to paper, I was simply trying to collect my thoughts, reflect upon the meaning of life, and discern my own identity. Slowly, I began to sense that my individual reflections were part of a huge, flowing stream of humanity, surging to become more human and more whole. Yes, we are all separate, we are all existentially alone; and yet somehow we are all connected, we are all one. But even in the experience of oneness we remain unique. We are not absorbed or obliterated. I found this paradox deeply rooted in all my thoughts, feelings, dreams, relationships, and prayers. The more I tried to focus on this reality, the broader became its dimensions, until I suddenly realized that when I am most celibate (most focused and centered, most who I am), I am also most passionate (most in love with God and with others).

Celibate Passion has not been an easy book to write, and I suspect that it will be a challenge to many readers. For it is a personal expression of faith and a painful probing of what it means to be in pursuit of wholeness. To be whole, I believe, is to be fully human and authentically religious. It is to burn intensely for integrity. It is to be engaged in loves that are as erotic as they are spiritual, as fleshy as they are ethereal. This wholeness defies the dualisms which have traditionally defined our existence. It somehow transcends all of life's contradictions; yet it mysteriously affirms and reconciles life's persisting intransigent polarities. This wholeness, which I call *celibate passion,* is the essence of what I dream and the integrity for which I long.

Celibate Passion is divided into ten chapters, the first of which is an introduction. Each of the subsequent chapters deals with a specific aspect of wholeness which I felt I must address: life, death, prayer, God, creativity, sexuality, intercourse, life-style, and religious experience. I still have questions about each of these topics. And I am quite sure that my understanding and present answers are but the beginning of a search I must continue. Nevertheless, I hope that what I write here will find resonance with you in some small way. From my solitude I reach out to affirm your solitude, whether you are male or female, lay or clergy, married or single, and I pray that our prayers for one another will encourage and enkindle us both to keep journeying into the fullness of celibate passion.

JANIE GUSTAFSON

❀ 1. MULTIPLE ONENESS

I A M a child of post–World War II America. All I have ever known is upheaval, transition, and change. Almost every possibility seems to have been packed into the last twenty-five years. I have seen the control of polio, the beginning of the space program, the renovation of inner cities, the rise of equal rights, the impact of oral contraceptives, and the deliberations of Vatican II. I have also known the violence of riots and civil conflict, the murder of national leaders, the disintegration of marriage, the legalization of abortion, and the removal of God from the public school system.

Like so many of my peers, I carry within me the full burden of what Alvin Toffler has termed "future shock." In the past eleven years I have moved a dozen times. My jobs have ranged from lab work in a hospital to teaching in elementary school, high school, and college. My family has been torn apart by drugs, alcohol, and divorce. Values I once held with clarity have now become clouded. Choices which once were simple have now become complex. Everywhere I look there is a wide spectrum of options from which to choose, and today's society tells me that all of the alternatives are good. My background, however, makes me a little suspicious. How many options can I really exercise? Just how much diversity can one body sustain? How shall I know if what I have chosen is really what my life is to be all about?

It seems I could spend my entire life drifting from one thing to the next, for each time I choose one option, it reveals a new set of possibilities. "One answer breeds a multitude of new questions; explanations are merely indications of greater puzzles."[1] But I am afraid of drifting. I want my life to have meaning, some direction, a goal. How I long for a yellow brick road which will lead me safely through this scrambled existence and into the city of Oz! But, alas, no such road will ever be part of my reality. Because of the confusion which surrounds me, I realize I must look within myself to find the answers I so desperately seek.

I am now discovering that in the midst of my fragmentariness, there lies a deep-seated life force. It is a passion for wholeness, for integrity, for oneness. I seek to end my alienation from the world. I long to penetrate life's secrets and uncover the roots of its mysteries. I yearn to free myself from all that is transitory, piecemeal, fractional. Like Anne Morrow Lindbergh, I want to be at peace with myself, with other people, and with God.

> I want a singleness of eye, a purity of intention, a central core to my life that will enable me to carry out these obligations and activities as well as I can . . . I want to live in "grace" . . . I am seeking what Socrates asked for in the prayer from the Phaedrus when he asked: "May the outward and inward . . . be at one."[2]

This passion races through my bloodstream and pulses with the thirst for harmony. I seek communion with my surroundings. I desire to find someone who can share my experiences and frustrations, my joys and dreams. I long for moments of intimacy, for in these moments, new feelings of strength and goodness fill my heart. I can forget all that is mundane and petty. I become inflamed by the present, and reconciliation of all my contradictory parts seems possible. I can embrace my own mystery and transcend the chaos within me. I can become myself the passion and, in so doing, become one with the universe.

This sense of oneness, however, needs further explanation. For this very same passion necessarily leads me to discover my utter uniqueness and solitariness. As *The Prophet* of Kahlil Gibran poignantly reminds me, intimacy requires individuality.

Sing and dance together and be joyous
but let each of you be alone.
Even as the strings of a lute are alone
though they quiver with the same music.
Stand together yet not too near together.
For the pillars of the temple stand apart
and the oak tree and the cypress
grow not in each other's shadow.[3]

The core of my existence is and always will be celibate. I alone am responsible to select my values and to shape my life. I am separate from the world around me and loved by God for who I am. Regardless of my oneness and union with another, there will always remain a distinct "me."

I have not always understood the two-sidedness of this passion. Sometimes, when I am overwhelmed by the pain and darkness of loneliness, I am aware only of the need to be united with another. The intensity of this drive can become so great that I understand why in the Upanishads and Shankara's Vedanta oneness with the Absolute is perceived as annihilation of the individual personality. Like the writers of those texts, I yearn to be caught up, possessed, permeated with God until I no longer exist. I want to completely enter him *(laya)* and become *(samya, tan-mayata, satmata)* what I behold, until distinctions of subject and object disappear. To appease this desire, I usually try to throw myself into my job, melt into a lover or friend, or identify with a cause. I may experience wholeness for a while, but soon the inner gnawing returns, and I realize the futility of my attempts. Only then do I remember that I am a unique expression of God's creation and that, precisely because of that uniqueness, I will always be alone.

Surprisingly enough, this uniqueness, or celibacy, is a value which I find emerging from the conglomerate of the past two decades. Certainly it is not the traditional religious form of celibacy but celibacy in its widest sense. Today, more and more people are remaining or becoming single. College and graduate study have prolonged the premarital years. Birth control pills, the rising divorce rate, and the women's liberation movement have all added to the increasing attractiveness of the single state. But the celibacy of which I am writing is not even limited to the condition of being unmarried. *Celibacy,* as I mean the term, is that dimension of me which can never be given away, exhausted, or comprehended. It is the embodiment of my fullest potential, my entire personality, the solitary "I" in any relationship. It is my integrated character, my interior freedom to love and to receive love.

Celibate passion, the simultaneous desire for union and for singularity, is indeed a paradox. In the very moment of union I am somehow given back to myself. Even in mystical union with God, in moments of prayer or in death, I remain uniquely myself. As Teilhard de Chardin writes: " . . . in the divine personality we shall inevitably find ourselves personally immortalized."[4] This oneness is comparable to the union of iron and fire, or salt and water. The two become one, yet they remain distinct. What I am discovering is that wholeness does not mean solely the experience of intimate fusion with another, but rather the precarious balance between such intimacy and my own uniqueness. For me, "oneness" has come to mean fidelity to this balance, and thus it is a oneness which I consider to be multiple.

Before the 1960s our society did not seem to value a oneness which preserved individuality. Oneness was defined solely in terms of conformity. In the secular world, there was great emphasis on the "in" style of dress, the "right" kind of haircut, the "best" brand of cigarettes, the "most luxurious" make of car. Job roles and sex roles were clearly defined. It was socially unacceptable to differ from these standards. Even within convents, all nuns looked alike, walked alike, and wrote with the same style of penmanship. Time-proven customs and schedules seldom changed for any circumstance or for any individual.

During the 1960s a tremendous shift occurred from conformity to pluralism, from absolutism to relativism. At a time in my life when peer pressure to conform should have been at its height, society began to stress the importance of individualism. From free-style dancing and "whatever goes" clothing, to the so-called "sexual revolution" and change in life-styles, the message rang loud and clear: to be unique is good. To do your own thing is OK. The religious renewal which flowed from Vatican II has reflected the same change in consciousness. I am just beginning, however, to see the real implications of such a change. I am being called to perceive God in all situations and in all choices. I am being challenged to tear down the stereotypes of the past and to flesh out my own definitions of religion, humanness, and sanctity. I am being asked to develop my own value system without demanding the same values of others. I am encouraged to be honest with myself and most fully celibate, while simultaneously supporting the integrity and otherness of those around me. My vocation, I am discovering, is no less than that of Theresa of Lisieux: to love everything and everyone.

Meeting this challenge is easier said than done. So often, I expect the persons I love to think, feel, and believe the same things I do. I forget that oneness is not necessarily sameness. To love is to respect others for who they are and not for how closely they conform to my own personality. Loving everything also means that I must have a broad vision. But how easily I settle into myopia. I sometimes emphasize togetherness to the exclusion of privacy, or vice versa. I may join a campaign to help migrant workers or to teach in the inner city, but then forget the need for active participation in liturgical worship or my need for silence. I may concentrate too much on my job or social contacts, and overlook my family or community. I erroneously think that passion means to live life in extreme measures. I forget the wisdom of Buddha's "Middle Way." Oneness is not "either" or even "both." It is a union which somehow transcends and yet allows for "both."

Partly because of my childhood training, I find myself thinking that after I eliminate all the imperfections and evils of my life, I will start to be holy. Often, I find myself dreaming of an ideal situation in which I will be able to live in perfect peace, love, and harmony. What this means, quite literally, is that I put off holiness or love until some future time. This is the point which Alan Watts makes when he writes that "by and large the Western culture is a celebration of the illusion that good may exist without evil, light without darkness, and pleasure without pain."[5] My ideal world is often a one-sided fantasy. I am now realizing that I cannot become whole until I embrace everything. Nor can I be most myself without living and loving life's contradictions. Perhaps it is time to direct my attention to the full message of the Bible: "As long as the earth lasts, sowing *and* reaping, cold *and* heat, summer *and* winter, day *and* night shall always be" (Gen. 8:22).

Celibate passion, with its inherent polarities and tensions, is not a concept which adherents of Western rationalism, Machiavellianism, or Freudianism can accept. Perhaps this is why so many of my contemporaries have turned to the religions of the East. In Taoism, celibate passion is described as the successive movement of two contraries, Yin and Yang. Yang represents light, heat, summer, strength, positiveness, sunshine, rising, fire, maleness. Yin connotes shade, smoke, darkness, cold, negativeness, weakness, yielding, winter, earth, femaleness. Though these principles are in tension, they are not flatly opposed. They complement and counterbalance each other. Each invades the other's hemisphere; each establishes itself in the very center of the other's territory.

Yin and Yang are implicitly one. As the ancient Chinese philosopher Lao Tzu tells us, "all things bear the shade (Yin) on their backs and the sun (Yang) in their arms."[6] Their blending brings harmony and equilibrium to the world. Chou Tun-yi, the father of neo-Confucianism, says that from their interaction the four seasons are born. Water, fire, wood, and metal are produced. Oneness is not only a balance between rest (Yin) and motion (Yang); each pole is the root from which the other springs.

The Eastern philosophies, however, are only partial approaches to truth. A different approach to celibate passion may be found in the Western Judeo-Christian polarity of *Ish* and *Esh*.[7] *Ish* is the Hebrew word for fire and *Esh* is the word for earth. These symbols show the interrelatedness of matter and energy in the world, and add a theistic dimension to Taoism's Yin and Yang. The Judeo-Christian God is the fire which consumes all matter and is, at the same time, the divine ground of all beings. As the American Jewish theologian Abraham Heschel believes, it is the interplay of Ish and

Esh, "the tension of the known and the unknown, of the common and the holy, of the nimble and the ineffable, that fills the moments of our insights"[8] and drives us to seek God. The passion of the divine ground within reaches out to encompass the eternal flame.

The mere reciprocity between Yin and Yang is not enough for the Judeo-Christian. Ish and Esh transcend Tao's impersonalism with a God who is both suprapersonal and personal. He is the one who embraces all and who sustains all as separate from himself. God is at once the Alpha and the Omega, our beginning and our destiny, the ultimate of creative activity and what T. S. Eliot called the "still point." This God is sufficient unto himself and yet continually relational. Because he far surpasses us and yet is our deepest self, this Western God calls us to a passion that is distinctly celibate. "Hear O Israel," cries the great Jewish *Shemah*. "You shall love the Lord your God with all your heart and with all your soul and with all your thought, and him only shall you serve" (Dt. 6:4–5).

Other Western philosophers have written about celibate passion in terms of a unity which sustains contradictions. Among these philosophers are St. Augustine, Boethius, Pseudo-Dionysius, St. Anselm, St. Bonaventure, and Meister Eckhart. Particularly impressive are the writings of the fifteenth-century Bishop Nicholas of Cusa, who believes that in God all opposites are maintained and yet reconciled in perfect oneness. "As the absolute maximum, God contains all things; he is their enfolding *(complicatio)* and their unfolding *(explicatio)*."[9] God is not this or that; he is everything and yet above everything. He is a multiple oneness.

How I perceive God has a direct bearing on how I perceive my world. In my yearning for some type of meaning and stability, I have often regarded him as the unchanging rock of Psalm 18. He has indeed been my refuge, my shelter, my support. I see now that in this perception I have limited God in all that he is, and I have divorced him totally from the changes I find around me. The real Judeo-Christian God has many different faces. In the first chapter of Genesis, God creates a world that is not only filled with diversity, but a world that is made in his image and likeness. "I am Yahweh, unrivaled," the prophet Isaiah reminds us. "I form the light and create the dark. I make good fortune and create the calamity; it is I, Yahweh, who do all this" (Is. 45:7).

In affirming a belief in monotheism, we easily forget about the completeness of God. In multiplicity he is the synthesis of all diversity; in oneness he is the preservation of all plurality. Out of chaos God makes meaning and creates unity. I think that today, more than ever before, we are being called to see the God of our environment and the God who is within. He is not to be limited to a church building, a Sunday liturgy, or even to a specific time of prayer. He comes to us in many ways: the clanging of a street car in San Francisco, the bumper-to-bumper traffic on the Santa Monica freeway, a political convention, a biology classroom, the smile of a stranger, a walk along Malibu's beach. As the Atharva Veda is teaching me, God is the one light which appears in numerous forms. He is there in the fire and here in my heart and yonder in the sunset. He is the thread which unites everything.

These thoughts about God stimulate me to look differently at my life. I no longer think of salvation as delivery from all evil, darkness, or contradictions. Rather, I think Jesus saves me by showing me how to deal with diversity. Humanness and divinity somehow coexist. Salvation is a reparation, a reconciliation, an atonement, or at-one-ment, of all opposites. Jesus' message beckons me to a passionate love for God and for my neighbors. His cross is both horizontal and vertical. To follow him, I must contain within my own body a union of multiplicity.

Herein lies my vocation, my own passion and death. And herein lies my dilemma. I often forget that the way to salvation must not only be in and through multiplicity, but that the goal itself is also a union which sustains multiplicity. It is in and through confusion, turmoil, and darkness that I will have to approach wholeness. I must learn to live with questions and absurdities, and realize that perhaps even in heaven I will still be baffled by life's mysteries.

But how do I attain this broader vision of reality? Celibate passion may be found in every religion and culture and may be reached through any of them. The Hindus call it *turiya*, a "pure, unitary consciousness, wherein awareness . . . of multiplicity is completely obliterated."[10] The Zen Buddhists call it *satori*, a moment in which "all the opposites and contradictions of the world are united and harmonized into a consistent organic whole."[11] Western mystics have spoken of it as "the spiritual marriage" in which the finite and the infinite, the flesh and the spirit are joined. Celibate passion is an attitude beyond any reasoning, a way of thinking in which "all disturbances caused by the intellect are harmonized in a unity of higher order."[12]

Celibate passion is more than a perceptive attitude toward life; it is a relentless drive to delve deep into what it means to be fully human. This does not mean that I have to change my church affiliation or look to another culture for all the answers. Instead it means stilling my interior turmoil so that it may be transformed into creative energy. It means finding my own identity and reaching wholeness by relating to others while remaining rooted in my own experience.

I do not expect that this journey toward wholeness will be easy. I will have to be simultaneously convinced and detached, universal and particular, contemplative and active, vehement and docile. As both Qoheleth and Jesus remind me, life contains times for fasting and times for feasting, times for observing the law and times for breaking it, times for being sexual and times for being virginal. To embrace all of these times, I will have to let go of my cherished opinions and my righteous attitudes. I will have to stop confining people, God, and life. I suspect that this conversion will not be grandiose or ostentatious. There will be no dynamic thunderclap or spectacular sign in the heavens. As with Hermann Hesse's Siddhartha, this change will probably occur after a long period of time; it will happen almost imperceptibly during my ordinary, day-to-day experiences. There will be nothing "but a preparation of the soul, a capacity, a secret art of thinking, feeling, and breathing thoughts of unity at every moment of life."[13]

One of the strongest thrusts of celibate passion is the desire to bring all things together. I believe we are most human and most like God when we exert efforts to reconcile the discordances of our world. To do this necessitates a vision which may seem insane. For we must refuse to accept contradictions as irresolvable and refuse to accept the choices we make as absolute or irrevocable. I do not believe that humanness can any longer be a matter of "eithers": life or death, good or bad, joy or suffering. Humanness, as well as sanctity, is a matter of all the alternatives. Each of us must be like Siddhartha's ferryman: a bridge, reaching out and connecting all that is separate. Full humanness embraces the vision of St. Paul: "There is no such thing as Jew or Greek, slave or free person, male or female, for they are all one" (Gal. 3:28).

Once we envision the possibility of unity, I believe we are commissioned to spend ourselves in bringing it about. Our full-ness must overflow into the emptiness and chaos of the world. We must somehow unite the realistic and mystic aspects of existence. To be human and in pursuit of God is to see the New Jerusalem, not as a distant future but as the same city, in which we are involved, the same and yet transformed and enhanced with divine possibilities. Inebriated by the God within and around us, I think we can transfigure our barren environments "into standing pools, and the parched land into springs of water" (Ps. 107:35). From the metropolitan wilderness can come fresh, abundant life, "the growth of cedars, acacias, myrtles, and olives" (Is. 41:19).

Filled with this vision, I no longer find today's many changes and contradictions so threatening. Assuredly, I do not expect life to get easier. I foresee growing pains, mistakes, and setbacks. But I am not as discouraged or apprehensive as I was before. Whole-ness, celibate passion, is possible. Encouraged by this belief, I can say with St. Paul that "I forget the past and I strain ahead for what is still to come" (Phil. 3:14). I can now look differently at the contradictions within me. And I can now begin to explore the first questions I must answer on this journey: What does it mean to be human? What purpose does my life have?

❧ 2. DESERT GARDEN

THE Baltimore Catechism taught me that the purpose of life is to know, love, and serve God. What this now means to me is that to be fully human is to be authentically religious—not "religious" in the sense of joining a vowed community of men or women, but "religious" in the sense of orienting one's life toward God. To me, religion must not only encompass the spiritual dimension of existence, but must embrace as well all that is human. Religion is not something which is otherworldly or out of touch with reality. It must be universal, earthy, and fully sensuous.

Exposure to numerous "religious" persons—various gurus, Hare Krishna followers, Mormon apostles, Hindu devotees, Unification Church "Moonies," and the like—has made me concerned about the quality of what we call "religion." Some of these supposedly religious people seem to be moving through life so gingerly that they do not know what real living is about. Like somnambulists, they go through the motions of walking, talking, eating, praying, and relating to others, but without being consciously or passionately present. Their minds seem to be tuned into a specific frequency (perhaps the Eastern Om, the chanted mantra, the Jesus prayer, or the Catholic rosary); they seem to live in another world. In a group, they tend to be conforming, rigidly structured, and oriented to the status quo. They are imaginative only within acceptable or traditional lines of thought; they are creative only in approved areas. They do not appear free to question, free to doubt, or free to disagree significantly.

I notice these people probably because I find the same tendencies within myself. And it frightens me that I could be content to limit my experience to a religion which seems to be so dispassionate and stagnant. I do not want my prayer to be a preoccupation which insulates me from the substance of living. I want to touch life and let it touch me; I want to be fully aware, responsive, and loving, immersed and grounded in the realities of this earth.

There are two main reasons, I think, why our society has produced so many lifeless religious people. First, we still regard religious training or formation as something which can be given. We rely on a program, a specific curriculum, a spiritual master, or a disciplined Church environment, to provide what we or our children need to be religious. Religion is something imposed from the outside. Implicit in this approach is a belief in a kind of Skinnerian psychology: that interior religious attitudes can be shaped by modifying external behavior. We thus come to depend on artificial support systems, and when they are removed or changed, we cannot stand on our own. We do not necessarily take responsibility for our own values or decisions. We can too easily go through the actions without internalizing any real beliefs.

Second, we have assumed that a certain set of attitudes, values, and customs are right, or are more right than others. If we do not hold these "correct" values prior to our religious education, we expect to acquire them. If we do hold these values, we expect religion to help us improve or maintain them. Behind this assumption lies another dualistic one. There is a bad "self" which must be whittled away to allow the "spirit" to gain the upper hand. The sacred differs from the secular; spirit is better than matter, and saintly perfection somehow overlooks our basic human condition.

Two facets of psychological conditioning present in religious training programs seem to prevent celibate passion from becoming part of our lives. The first type of conditioning opposes humility to pride. This interpretation of humility causes us to regard anything which concerns our "selfhood" or "ego" as bad. We find ourselves immersed in sin, and nothing we do can ever be enough to redeem us. We are saved only through the infinite mercy of God. Consequently, we may suppress our genuine feelings, deny our deepest thoughts, and never come to know our real selves. Because we judge ourselves as proud, self-indulgent, and full of ambition, we do not affirm our basic goodness or believe that God can be within us.

What often happens in this first dualism is that we begin to identify our faults, inefficiencies, or mistakes with sin. We feel guilty about our imperfections. In the quest for sainthood, we may overzealously attempt to transcend our humanness, or like Judas, we may give up altogether in guilt and despair. In either case, there is no self-acceptance, and we continue to condemn not only these defects in ourselves but similar ones in others.

In this dualism, pride is often equated with self-assertion, flamboyancy, and exhibitionism. We are to model our lives on the poor Publican instead of the rich Pharisee. We should pray in secret, perform our tasks quietly, and never look for rewards or praise. We should consider our talents and abilities examples of pride, and thus we may repress or seek to hide them. We may never assume leadership roles in our church, our community, or our educational systems. We may simply sit back and go along, perhaps mumbling, but never loud enough for anyone else to hear.

The second type of conditioning which I feel has inhibited our realization of celibate passion is the insistence that authority and obedience are opposed to autonomy and independence. One of the important trademarks of religious training is the omnipotent "will of God." This is an absolute which cannot be challenged or questioned, and for some reason, always resides outside of ourselves. We are taught to listen to the will of God as expressed through peers, superiors, or the Church. To be "religious," we must obey with docility. Directly opposed to this concept of holiness is any manifestation of self-determination. We are not to solely follow the voices within us, for they may lead us in the wrong direction. Here, conformity is more virtuous than individuality.

This duality may lead us to overemphasize security. We may develop (or accept from others) whole systems of structures, patterns, and rules which are dependable and safe. We seek reasons for everything and are afraid of unanswerable questions. We fastidiously plan out the future while avoiding too close a look at the present situation. We feel helpless to bring about change, and therefore we gradually stop entertaining doubts or criticisms. We settle for traditional ways, and religion deteriorates into a businesslike organization. Safety becomes more valuable than risk or experimentation.

It does not surprise me that so many people today are turned off by religion. It is not healthy to always maintain the status quo, or to be so influenced by the opinions of others that we cannot venture to explore and discover life for ourselves. Nor is it appropriate to be bound to a vision that is so dualistic that we can affirm only half of reality. We are not fully human if our beliefs keep us infantile or adolescent. After sixteen years of religious education and four years of religious formation, I am only now beginning to discern what I value and to acknowledge what I feel. I am just starting to feel free to question my beliefs, to test, to doubt, and to experiment in my expressions of them. I am just beginning to allow myself to feel angry or jealous, happy or proud.

Daily, I find myself being called to transcend the dualisms of my religious training and to become more aware of the many possibilities in life. This call seduces me to shed layer upon layer of my safe, comfortable facade. I must let life in. I must fill myself with all that is God and even more ardently desire his presence. I must empty myself to others, in tears and kisses, in hugs and smiles. Celibate passion does not just happen. To attain it, I must care and be responsible; I must hurt and I must bleed. I must undergo a slow process of transformation, like that of a seed germinating in the earth.

Surprisingly enough, this call to be more human and more religious has made me even more appreciative of my Judeo-Christian background. I have discovered in the desert journey of the Israelites my own life journey. My journey may not be through the physical desert of Moses, John the Baptist, or Charles de Foucauld, but it is an experience of place, time, and movement. This experience invites me to enter the desert of my own heart, to uncover the dark, hidden recesses of my deepest self. It calls me to face this self, my God, and other people. It challenges me to face solitude and loneliness, to acknowledge my innate celibacy, to be stripped, to be opened up, and, despite all my sinfulness, infidelity, and ugliness, to be loved.

Every time I go to Arizona I am struck by the desert's stark contrast to my usual forms of retreat and my "normal" classes of religious instruction. Most of the time, whether in the classroom or in a retreat house, I choose structures and schedules that provide a great deal of stability to the day. Usually I opt for a passive, sedentary role, either as a student or as a church member. What I think at the time is a real prayer experience is usually, in retrospect, a mere flight of fancy or intellect. When the course ends, when the retreat is over, I return to my everyday existence and find that nothing within or around me has changed. I am no more "religious" or alive than when I started. I am simply more immersed in the snares of my dualistic thinking.

Real living is never a safe thing. There are no structures or schedules. Life makes no promises and sets no deadlines. It is a tremendous risk, with no guarantee of success. It is as wild and unpredictable as an LSD trip, which can lead us into ecstasy or crash us brutally into hell. Anyone who has taken a wilderness survival course knows that life in the wild is a struggle which demands an intense, whole-bodied involvement. You cannot just be spiritual; you have to be earthy. You have to get your hands dirty; you have to plan ahead and be alert at all times. You have to conserve food and make sure there is enough fuel. You cannot afford to be unrealistic, for the wilderness will not hesitate to kill you.

Three years ago, I decided that I could no longer continue living as I had been. My life was nice and respectable, but much too sheltered, dualistic, and unreal. I wanted to be whole. I wanted to discern a path for my life's journey. I wanted to grow closer to

God. And so I went, not to the physical desert, but to the wilderness. I lived by myself in an old weathered log cabin deep in the woods of Nova Scotia. Around me was a community of men and women hermits, who came together twice a day for prayer and about three times a week for meals. I stayed there for eight months, through the mosquito-infested summer, the gorgeously colored fall, and the dark, frozen winter. It was an experience that altered me in ways no other situation has.

What made this wilderness experience so different from my previous forms of religious education? Perhaps this. The desire to understand myself and my life's purpose became so urgent that I *had to go* to the wilderness. Nova Scotia lured me. And instead of listening to my head with its usual logical abstractions, I listened to my heart. Like Jesus who was *driven* into the desert, I was seized by an irresistible passion to really know life with every fiber of my being. In the past, I had never been driven to such extremes. I had been content to automatically follow the items on my prearranged agenda. I see now that I went too fast and too casually to my religion classes, retreats, and liturgies, and I think this is partly why they failed to enliven me.

Jesus spent thirty years in preparation before he went to the desert. When I first went to the wilderness, I thought I had gone there for the right reasons, and I thought I was prepared. But looking back now, I see how little I understood the meaning of that call, and how poorly equipped I was to deal with what I found there. I went to the woods to live more simply, but I brought everything with me; not just external possessions, but my hopes, fears, needs, wants, memories, sins, and imperfections. Most of all, I brought my old patterns of thinking and all the dualisms of my previous training. I was much like Abraham in this regard. When he was called by God into the desert, he simply transported himself, his family, and all his possessions to a new environment. He did not leave anything behind; he just moved. God worked on Abraham through the years, however, and slowly refined him until his past modes of living and believing had been removed. Abraham had a difficult time of it, and rightly so, because God had to empty him of his former understanding of life before filling him with new purpose.

This seems to be the pattern of the desert. And this is why I think it teaches humility as no other type of religious training can. We think we are so wise and so versed in the ways of life, and then the harshness of the wilderness tells us how presumptuous we have been. The same thing happened to Abraham's descendants. They either wanted to get right to the Promised Land, or they wanted to return to the safety of Egypt. God had to spend forty years chiseling, polishing, and purifying them of their ancient ideologies. I guess I should not have expected my own perfection to take place in a shorter time. Nova Scotia indeed stripped me, but it took much longer than I ever dreamed or planned on. Three years later, I am still being stripped and emptied.

The book of Kings reminds me that Elijah's experience of life is no different. As a prophet, he thinks he can get through life on his own abilities—that is, until he smashes the idols of the people and they try to kill him. Elijah then runs to the desert. There, he learns that only God can sanctify our earthenware bodies; only he can unite matter and spirit; only he can make us fully human. But how God will accomplish this will always appear strange and mysterious. His answer is never an answer but a summons to further questioning and further journeying. Elijah, without answers, must return to Damascus and continue searching.

The desert can shock us out of old patterns of thinking because it imposes upon us a rigid asceticism. Controlled sensory deprivation has always been an important method of breaking through to new realms of consciousness. Fasting can increase our intuitive powers, teach us self-discipline, make us more sensitive to others and aware of our utter dependence on God's grace. The problem, however, with prolonged sensory deprivation or a rigorously disciplined methodology of religious conduct, is that the asceticism or discipline can itself become the end instead of the means. We can get so engrossed in the physical dimension of what we are doing that we lose sight of the spiritual. Or, just the opposite, we can come to view the sensual as bad, as something which needs to be obliterated before we can be holy.

Experience of numerous Eastern and Western communities that emphasize a meatless diet, two hours of yoga per day, and various other rituals has led me to realize that the more disciplined life is not necessarily the more religious life. Jesus himself was no ascetic, although he did value discipline and he did sometimes live ascetically. If I engage in asceticism for its own sake, I do not automatically become more conscious of God. There can be a subtle temptation in gaining full mastery over one's body. The tendency is to say, "Look what I have done!" or even worse, "Because I can do this, I must be holy." Personal pride or self-satisfaction is the most crippling road block to being religious. Instead of encouraging me to look at myself, the real desert challenges me to say: "Look what God is doing, in, through, and with me."

The asceticism I found in Nova Scotia was extremely demanding. Because there was no electricity, I could not switch on a light or listen to a record or iron my clothes. Instead of vacuuming, I had to sweep; instead of using mixers, blenders, and sewing machines, I had to beat ingredients and mend clothes by hand. Because there was no running water during the winter, I found myself tramping through the snow to the partially frozen well to fetch water for drinking, cooking, and bathing. Because there was no consistent source of heat, each winter night became a feat of survival in sub-zero temperatures. Because I lived alone and because there was no phone, it was usually days before I saw or talked with another person.

This sensory deprivation had several effects on me. First, it made me acutely appreciative of many aspects of ordinary modern living. I came to value electricity, running water, warmth, and friendship as never before. Second, the asceticism stretched me to my limits. Life, with all its insecurities, pounded at me until I felt raw. Everything I did, from chopping down trees, to driving a tractor, to raising a pig, was not only a new experience, but a huge risk. Like St. Paul, I could no longer ignore my own vulnerability. Being in the wilderness was terrifying because it brought me face to face with the demonic powers inside myself, powers which could be angelic or evil, creative or destructive. I often found myself complaining to God in words similar to those of the Israelites. "Why did I not stay in California where I was able to live comfortably? As it is, you have brought me to this wilderness to kill me" (compare Ex. 16:3).

One of the most persistent demons during my stay in Nova Scotia was the thought that I was wasting my time. So much of my day was taken up with the tasks of survival that I was not reading, writing, or praying any more than in my former city environment. This demon told me there was so much good I could be doing elsewhere, in my chemistry classroom in San Francisco, in the parish in Phoenix, or in some place I hadn't even been yet. The discipline of the wilderness no longer seemed reasonable, the asceticism lost its meaning. I wanted to run away from those woods and walk among people again. I wanted to stop the howling inner demons whose voices penetrated deep into the marrow of my bones.

Sensory deprivation stripped me of all my defenses against life. I came close to complete despair. Wholeness could not possibly be found in that leaky log cabin or in that endless cold. Life seemed to have no purpose at all. My faults seemed so horrible as to be unredeemable. I felt no assurance that I was making any spiritual progress, nor could I envision an end to my misery. It was then then I realized the psychic dimensions of my earlier religious training. In these woods I had fallen into the same trap of dualistic thinking. I was hugging a self-concept which labeled me as bad, and I was groping to maintain some sense of dependence and security.

This realization initiated tremendous changes in me. The wilderness asceticism deliberately pruned me and sharpened my perception of myself. As I began to recognize my own creatureliness, I also began to comprehend my vast need for God's presence. I could live without electricity, without indoor plumbing, and to a certain extent, without other people. But I could not live without God. To be fully alive, I had to have a solid relationship with him. The wilderness taught me to find God everywhere, even in the mundane tasks of everyday living.

In this, I was much like St. Paul. As the Acts of the Apostles recounts, he is so full of his own determination to be holy that God has to knock him down to get him to see the truth. Only then does Paul realize how vulnerable he is and how many defenses he has manufactured to hide his inner fragility. Some time after this experience, he writes to the Corinthians of his need for God: "To stop me from getting too proud, I was given a thorn in the flesh, an angel of Satan to beat me. About this thing I have pleaded for it to leave me, but God has said: 'My grace is enough for you; my power is at its best in your weakness'" (2 Co. 12:7–9). Knowledge of our own weaknesses certainly fosters humility. Paul learns his lesson well and becomes, in the process, more human and more saintly.

The realization of my need for God also has made me appreciate first-hand the ancient wisdom of the Jewish religion. The Old Testament reiterates over and over again that the Hebrews are a people doomed to fail continually. Theirs is such a demanding code of conduct, with laws to govern every minute detail of life, that they cannot possibly keep the entire law. The Israelites will always fail in some way. What this constant failure does is to call these people again and again to re-examine the meaning of life. Jesus condemns the Pharisees for their insistence on the possibility of achieving perfection through the law. They are so caught up in external observances that they have forgotten their need for God's reconciling grace.

I think a stance of profound neediness for God is particularly hard to arrive at in today's society. We have so many comforts; we can do so many things. Because our technology has become so sophisticated, we can live quite well without prayer and without God. We have pushed God to the periphery because we have not really needed him. It is only when we try to grapple with questions of meaning and purpose that we realize our utter emptiness without God. Only in times of crisis, when we realize our old answers are quite inadequate and our ancient gods have been shattered, must we wait for God to come.

Waiting is not valued by our culture. And this is another reason why so much of our religious training is so lacking. We do not fully appreciate that "the only way to know God is to go to him in humility, simplicity, and poverty, entering his silence, and there in prayer and patience, waiting until he reveals himself."[1] We do not wait long enough. Eight days or one semester may be long enough to rejuvenate some people, but not for me. I simply cannot predict the time or place when God will speak to me. There are some things in life I cannot control or plan or manipulate. They just happen, and until then, I must wait. Perhaps this is the reason why Joseph had to spend time at the bottom of a cold dark well before he was sold to the Egyptians. Or maybe it is the reason why Jonah spent time in the belly of a whale before proceeding to Ninevah, or why Jesus spent time in the tomb before the resurrection. Waiting helps me clarify what I believe. It forces me to surrender and accept the limitations of my clay body.

If I wait long enough, God does come. And in his coming, my complaints are silenced, my fears are dispelled, and I am healed. Gaining self-knowledge and then self-acceptance is the most important task in the journey of becoming whole. However much time it takes to accomplish this is never time wasted. I am beginning to see that I cannot run away from my needs, doubts, and questions about the purpose of my life. These questions travel with me and force me again and again to face the darkness within. But it is precisely through the darkness, in my weakness and sin, that I will discover God.

To me, humility now means that while knowing my limitations, I must acknowledge the dignity of my earthiness. Obedience means that I must listen to my own inner voices as well as those of others, and that I must accept full responsibility for my beliefs and my destiny. To be religious and to be earthy must be one and the same. Life is a continual journey toward such integration. To become whole, I must let God strip me of dualistic misconceptions. Only through this emptying can I find purpose and meaning. Only then can life's desert become a garden.

The quest for wholeness requires a life-long commitment to being emptied. How much am I willing to give to this endeavor? How empty will I allow myself to become? How much do I really want to grow?

❧ 3. FLAMING PHOENIX

Are you willing to be sponged out, erased, cancelled,
made nothing?
Are you willing to be made nothing?
dipped into oblivion?
If not, you will never really change.
The phoenix renews her youth
only when she is burnt, burnt alive, burnt down
to hot and flocculent ash . . .
                                      —D. H. Lawrence[1]

THE most real aspect of living, Teilhard de Chardin believes, is
the passion for growth.[2] Always there is the inner surge to know
more about everything. We burn with curiosity; we are attracted
to the novel. We yearn for more truth and we beg for more experience. But as we noted in the last chapter, growing never takes place
without dying. The phoenix rises from the ashes of her own annihilation. But because we fear death, we also fear growing. We tend
to evade the truth about ourselves. We would rather gloss over the
fact that our bodies will someday decay and disintegrate.

I think this fear is what prevents us from coming to terms with
the celibate part of ourselves. To be celibate is to acknowledge that
each of us will die. Celibacy denies all of the historical myths of
immortality. We do not live on in our children or in our children's
children. Our seed or our life does not continue in this world

forever. Whether there is anyone left alive to remember or worship us is irrelevant. We live, and then we die. And we always face
death alone.

The author of Genesis considers death to be a punishment for
the sin of Adam and Eve. The biologist in me believes that death
has always been a part of the natural world. Perhaps there was a
time, however, when primitive peoples did not know that they
themselves would die. Growth in self-consciousness and knowledge, which is what the Genesis story is really about, inevitably
leads to the discovery of death. Everyone and everything dies.
Once we realize this, we must spend the rest of our days confronting death. Like Adam and Eve, we cannot go back to the lost
garden of ignorance. Things change and we move on. Nothing is
sacred or permanent.

Who are we? What are we? These questions about personal
identity have plagued men and women for centuries. On the one
hand we are little less than the gods. As Psalm 8 reminds us, we
are crowned with glory; we have dominion over the earth. On the
other hand, we are, in the words of St. Catherine of Siena, "an
abyss of nothing." We are paradoxical. We are split in two. We
are aware of our beauty and wonderful uniqueness, but we are also
aware that all the money and embalming fluid in the world cannot
prevent our extinction. Erich Fromm says we are half animal and
half symbol. Abraham Maslow is more graphic; he says we are half
God and half worm. We can soar to the heights of altered states
of consciousness, but we are continually limited by the physical
Esh of our bodies. In the words of the seventeenth-century mystic,
Blaise Paschal, we occupy a middle position in the universe; we are
"all in relation to nothingness and a nothingness in relation to all."
Our identity eludes us.

Nothingness is a word existentialists have used to describe the
anxiety-provoking dread that lies in the pit of the stomach when
we acknowledge that we will surely die. It is the feeling of incon-
gruity and of powerlessness before time and the forces of nature.
In essence, it is the fear of death itself as something irrational,
absurd, untimely, and impersonal. Michael Novak describes this

nothingness as "an experience beyond the limits of reason. It arises near the borderline of insanity. It is terrifying."[3] Others may die around us, but it is only with great panic and anguish that we comprehend the fact of our own mortality. To a slight degree, this nothingness is the constant uneasiness I feel living in Southern California, knowing that a major earthquake is due. To a greater degree, it is the overwhelming fear I once experienced when a violent storm almost stranded me overnight, alone and without supplies, in the middle of the Nova Scotian forest.

Existential nothingness, as T. S. Eliot notes in "Ash Wednesday," tears us apart bone by bone; it scrapes out all the substance we once had and discards it thoughtlessly over the earth. Nature pays no heed to human pleas or cajolings. Our plans, hopes, and future dreams are all met by silent indifference. Whether we are the poorest of the poor or as wealthy as was Howard Hughes, our fate is the same. Death comes. And before that, we suffer. "Pull me up from the depths of the earth," cries the psalmist (Ps. 71:20). "I am about to fall and my pain is always with me" (Ps. 38:17). "I lift my eyes to your mountain. When shall help come to me?" (Ps. 121:1). "You see my suffering; you know my trouble. Sorrow has shortened my life; weeping has reduced my years" (Ps. 31:-7,10).

Implicit in the dread of nothingness is the fear of condemnation. We recognize our dirtiness; we are afraid of our sinfulness and guilt. We stand naked, explosed, vulnerable. We are feeble, finite and fragile. We fear the wrath of God and the anger of our fellow beings. We know the prophecies of Hosea are all too true. God will indeed strip us down and expose us as on the day we were born. He will make a wilderness of us and leave us barren (see Ho. 2:2–3). We are merely clay vessels which he can smash as he pleases (see Si. 33:13). Before him we are helpless. All too easily, as he did to Job, God can exterminate our families, our enterprises, and our worlds.

The existential experience involves our entire being and often leaves us frustrated. No longer sure of our footing, we search high and low for solid ground, for something to hang on to, for something to identify with, for someone who can tell us who we are. We have a sneaking suspicion that someone must know our identity and our meaning. We become obsessed with finding ourselves. Try as we may to find ourselves in the passionate embrace of a lover, in the frenzied competition of a job, or in a life of moral perfection, our identities remain a mystery. We are forced to keep searching or to give up in despair.

Because we must know who we are, the existentialists say we are condemned to search. According to Jean-Paul Sartre, our desire for meaning, for identity, for unity with another will always remain unfulfilled. Never satisfied with the answers we find, we must continue to look. Even mystics of various religious traditions, when facing the abyss of nothingness, perceive its unanswerableness and its endlessness. "The more I enter, the more I find," writes Catherine of Siena, "and the more I find, the more of you I seek. You are the food that never satiates, for when my soul is satiated in your abyss, it is not satiated, but ever continues to hunger and thirst for you."[4]

The existentialists tell us to face nothingness with great courage; the Judeo-Christian tradition calls us to great faith. But either way, the message is the same. To be human means to come to terms with earthiness: death, emptiness, meaninglessness, and guilt. We must go beyond the ashes of despair in search of our true selves. Like Socrates, we must accept death as part of our being. Like the phoenix, we must rise to immortality by passing through the fires of nonexistence.

After much agonizing, I have come to realize the importance of confronting my own death. I agree wholeheartedly with Martin Heidegger's position in *Being and Time*. He believes we can achieve wholeness only when, in dread and silence, we face nothingness and shape our lives from the darkness of that encounter.[5] St. John of the Cross is even more emphatic: "In order to become everything, desire to be nothing."[6] I find myself asking, however, just what John of the Cross means by *nothingness*. It is the same nothingness that Heidegger writes about? Is it the gnawing anxiety I feel when I think about myself in a coffin? Is it the fear that my life may end there? Is it the horror that my life may be like a broken record, going around and around and never getting anywhere?

Perhaps the existentialist use of the word *nothingness* has confused my understanding of spiritual and psychological growth, but I no longer think that the nothingness of existential dread, darkness, and isolation is the same nothingness described by John of the Cross. The nothingness of the nineteenth-century philosophers and of Novak's *Experience of Nothingness* is an anguished dark night which is very much an experience of something. I am beginning to think that this dark night is a *preliminary* experience to that of real nothingness. Real nothingness is perhaps impossible to define, for it cannot even be the place where no thing is. Nothingness cannot be identified with anything, for then it ceases to be nothing. What I think John of the Cross attempts to do is lead us through and beyond our existential dread right up to the mountaintop of nothingness. *Nada, nada, nada,* and on that mountain, nothing.

John of the Cross sums up the experience of nothingness in a single sentence: "The soul must be in all its parts reduced to a state of emptiness, poverty, and abandonment, and must be left dry, empty, and in darkness."[7] To arrive at this state we will indeed know Novak's terror and loneliness. But once we have arrived, there will be nothing at all. The anguish of existential dread purifies us until finally nothing stands between us and God, "not even the most delicate of veils," as Nikos Kazantzakis says.[8]

It is extremely important to distinguish between existential anxiety (the philosopher's nothingness) and the experience of nothingness. This, to me, seems to be one of the most important jobs of a spiritual director. Real nothingness leads me to a fresh, vibrant freedom and a dynamic creativity. My Esh and Ish somehow get together. I am made whole. Emptiness, poverty, and abandonment take on new meaning. To be poor is to live with insecurity. To be empty is to accept myself as separate and distinct from everything and everyone else. To know abandonment is to let go, not only of the crutches and the superficial answers, but of the very feelings of fear. In nothingness, I willingly admit my celibacy; I joyfully stand apart from others as a unique being.

When I experience moments of real nothingness, I love to risk and to adventure. Each day is a new surprise. All my careful calculations fade away, and the present situation inebriates me. The ridiculous delights me and no dream seems farfetched. I am driven to break through the boundaries of my present condition. I continually blaze new trails, despite questions, opposition, or inner darkness. There is within me a faith that is stronger than absurdity, that urges me to transcend all limits and to expand all horizons.

Interestingly enough, when I am nothing, I am neither good nor bad. I cannot have a positive self-concept or a negative one. Instead, I have what the Zen Buddhists would call "no mind." There is no self-concept at all. I am totally self-oblivious and fully absorbed in whatever I am doing. Consequently, I experience exhilarating freedom and timeless immortality. There is an unconscious self-respect and integrity, because God really dwells within. And since he is continually creative, I simply usher his artistry into the world. I become transparent. No longer do I imprison myself or stifle his creative energy within me.

Distinguishing between existential anxiety and the experience of nothingness is a necessary first step in any type of spiritual or psychological growth. But it remains precisely that, a first step. Discernment is not authentic unless it leads to a consequent action. Jesus, in the ninth chapter of St. John's Gospel, insists that once we have discerned, we must act in accordance with our new knowledge. Perhaps this is why I have so much trouble distinguishing between anxiety and nothingness. It is not nothingness which hurts; what pains me is knowing that to arrive at nothingness, I must be "sponged out, erased, and cancelled" like D. H. Lawrence's phoenix. To grow and to change, as John of the Cross states, "is not only night and darkness for the soul, but is likewise affliction and torment."[9]

To accept pain willingly is never easy. In fact, if I think something is going to cause me great discomfort, I often prefer to avoid it. And sadly enough, almost everything in society, from its analgesic philosophy to its technological pursuit of pleasure, supports my avoidance. I have learned that it is wrong to feel empty or in pain. Whenever I feel the twinges of the anxiety that could lead me to nothingness, I instinctively repress it. I thereby close myself to passion. I cut off further possibilities.

To become whole, we must be able to distinguish between anxiety and nothingness, and also be able to understand how we respond to existential anxiety. The following diagram summarizes the conflicts which I believe we all experience in coming to understand who we are and the nature of death.

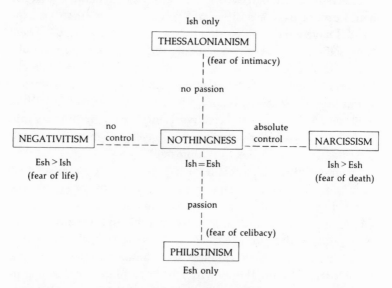

FIG. 1. Responses to Existential Anxiety

One reaction to existential anxiety is what Kierkegaard calls *philistinism*. This means mediocre existence, living in the security of the womb, satisfaction with everything as it is. It means to live life on the surface and to never explore its deeper psychic dimensions. It is the refusal to be born, the refusal to grow. This stance, I believe, is based on the fear of celibacy, the fear to stand alone, or to just be. As exhibited in the paranoia of Chief Bromden in *One Flew Over the Cuckoo's Nest,* philistinism is the fear to stick out too far. Kierkegaard describes this reaction as choosing to live in "half-obscurity."[10] It means being close-minded to passion, risk, and broader perspectives. It is a state of "shut-upness"[11] in which inauthentic people avoid the questions of personal meaning and death. Of people with these characteristics, Ernest Becker writes: "They follow out the styles of automatic and uncritical living. . . . They are one-dimensional. . . . totally immersed in the fictional games being played in their society."[12] They are the Acutes on Nurse Ratched's mental ward, content to go along with the system in their tranquil, lobotomized condition.

Philistinism, with its daily routine of repressed living, is a complete immersion in the Esh of existence to the denial of the Ish. We deny that we are paradoxical creatures, both matter and spirit. We define life only in terms of the job, the bank account, the vacation, the car, the family, and never find time to deal with more serious realities. Physical satisfaction is the end-all and be-all. If we just had enough money and the right technology, we could make death go away forever. Like the ancient Romans, we do not worry about tomorrow because it is today that counts. If we don't feel quite right, we can always take another pill, swallow some more bourbon, or have sex with someone exciting.

Directly opposed to philistinism is another reaction to anxiety which I call *thessalonianism.* This reaction is a type of mediocrity based on the fear of intimacy. Here, we are afraid to become involved with another. We are afraid of doing, and would rather remain detached and disinterested. Thessalonianism is an obsession with holiness that overlooks the present moment for the future. It is an otherworldliness that is apathetic toward physical reality, that ignores social issues such as injustice, poverty and hunger.

In thessalonianism, prayer can be a defense mechanism against building community with others. It is a position which acknowledges only the Ish of reality. The spirit is more important than matter. My personal relationship with God is all that concerns me.

Real, live people are distractions from my endeavors to be holy. In this stance, we believe in saving souls, but not in alleviating physical suffering, misery, or oppression.

Narcissism, a third reaction to anxiety, involves an attempt to gain control over reality. It is a love of self which fears annihilation or extinction. There are healthy amounts of this orientation in all of us, which contribute to feelings of self-worth and self-esteem. We all, to a certain degree, have the need to feel special and, on occasion, to be "number one." Taken to an extreme, however, narcissism becomes an impetuous flight of aggression and assertion, a violent Oedipal project, in which we seek to conquer death by becoming the creator and sustainer of our own lives. The creature in us usurps the Creator. We want to be God.

Narcissism seems to blind us to the consequences of control. We want to control life and death, but we balk at the idea of someone else controlling our existence. This is why I found the shock treatments and the frontal lobotomy forced on the main character of *One Flew Over the Cuckoo's Nest* so appalling. I once thought that I would much rather choose my death than have an unpredictable death happen to me. I now regard suicide as a narcissistic delusion. Even in suicide, death happens to us. To commit suicide is not an act of heroism in which we face death bravely. It is a last stand of narcissistic pride in a futile attempt to gain control.

It is almost impossible for us not to be narcissists. We want to be in control. As Ernest Becker points out:

> We don't want to admit that we are fundamentally dishonest about reality, that we do not really control our own lives. We don't want to admit . . . that we always rely on something that transcends us, some system of ideas and powers in which we are embedded and which support us.[13]

To insist on such control, we raise ourselves to a position of primary importance. Ish dominates Esh. A balance is upset. In Fromm's schema, our symbolic side tyrannizes our animal side. In Maslow's terminology, we make ourselves God and forget that we are worms. A person locked into this mentality can very easily

become schizophrenic. The symbolic self grows to such proportions that it cannot be contained in earthenware limits. The attempt to be a creator or a great saint ultimately destroys the whole
personality.

Directly opposed to narcissism is the experience of *negativism.* In
this reaction to existential anxiety, we feel that we have no control
over reality. We are discouraged and depressed by life. We fear to
really live. We cling to the bars of prisons we ourselves have
fashioned and feel that nothing we can do will ultimately make
any difference. Abraham Maslow has called this experience "the
Jonah Syndrome." Sigmund Freud called it a "castration complex."
It is characterized by the fear of realizing our fullest powers. Spe-
cifically, negativism cultivates feelings of inferiority, evil, and
shame, as defenses against full participation in life and full responsibility for our own beliefs.

Negativism may be considered the mirror image of narcissism,
for in this experience, self-preservation is again all important.
Here, as Novak points out, we are preoccupied with inventing our
"self," even if it is a negative one. Such negativism can paralyze
us with our own depression and can lead to full-blown psychosis.
Everything is regarded as a vanity of vanities. Esh dominates Ish.
The animal side crushes the symbolic self. We become acutely
aware of our isolation from others. Once we are locked into this
position, suicide seems to be the only way out. But again, as with
narcissism, even this is not a hero's way. It remains a final assertion
of one's guilt and personal worthlessness; it is a refusal to grasp
the entire truth.

All of us are products of our society, and consequently, we carry
within ourselves elements of philistinism, thessalonianism, narcissism, and negativism. These elements war against each other and
prevent us from entering fully into the dynamics of celibate passion. When we are immersed in philistinism, we are passionate in
the wrong way; in thessalonianism, we are too celibate. When
negativism surrounds us, we give up trying; when narcissism en-
gulfs us, we pursue only our own self-aggrandizement. Whatever
our response to anxiety, whatever our situation of unfreedom, we

generally choose to stay there. We do not enter the nothingness required for celibate passion.

In rereading the Gospels, I am just discovering one of the most important aspects of Jesus' ministry. He constantly challenges us to discern en route between our usual responses to anxiety and the nothingness required for more advanced stages of growing. With the Samaritan woman at the well, Jesus does not hesitate to say what he thinks. His frankness so startles this woman that she faces herself honestly. No longer can she live as before, in self-deception. Jesus' dialogue with Nicodemus has the same impact. Nicodemus is a good man, but Jesus confronts him emphatically: "Unless you are born again, you cannot enter the kingdom of God" (Jn. 3:5). These words not only stimulate new thoughts within Nicodemus; they lead him to change his life.

To move from where we are to the experience of nothingness is to move with passion, passion that is as monumental as the life of Jesus. This passion is not an obsession to control or to be controlled. It is a humble recognition that we do not have control over life and death, but that we are still responsible for what happens in life. This passion encourages us to remove our repressions, to discard our defenses, and to face death as inevitable. It is the passion to grow and to forever stamp out routine, automatic, or excessively self-confident activity.

It takes a tremendous amount of courage to find meaning in death, and it takes even more courage to stand apart from a society that idolizes youth, denies the fact of aging, and sugar-coats death with "resting in peace" or "passing away." When Jesus cures the blind man in John's Gospel, he not only frees him from personal blindness but frees him from his former religious beliefs, societal taboos, and social pressures. Jesus leaves this man with a vision that is so clear that it is the blind man himself who can tell the Pharisees they are on the wrong road (refer to Jn. 9:27).

It is not really surprising to me that our society is hard on its artists, contemplatives, musicians, and elderly. In my view, these groups of people, more than any others, continually challenge us to face the void within ourselves. They are to our society what the blind man was to the Pharisees. Their honesty forces us to be honest. Their refusal to ignore the fact of death challenges us to discover the real truth about ourselves. Their creativity evokes creativity within us. They hold up mirrors which remind us that continual discernment, conversion, and movement are still needed. Time is passing, and we have yet to arrive at full human-ness. We had better hurry before death comes. This is hardly a message we want to hear. Like the Pharisees of Jesus' time, we would much rather pretend that we are all that we should be.

We cannot bear too much truth at once. Just as Pilate has to wash his hands of Jesus, we too find ingenious ways to destroy those who are blatantly honest. By subtly changing a person's experience of nothingness to one of philistinism, thessalonianism, narcissism, or negativism, we can inhibit the very creativity which challenges us to change. Thus, we treat the artist as egotistical and selfish, or we label the musician impractical and undutiful. We scorn the contemplative as lazy, and we regard the elderly person as unproductive. Once we have convinced these persons that such identifications are true, the battle is won. Nothingness degenerates into some other reaction to anxiety. Creativity is stifled.

In my own case, nothingness most often degenerates into nega-tivism. This has been one of my biggest struggles as a writer and composer. Once I am stuck in the quicksand of negativism, I am in hell. I burn, suffer, die, but am immobilized. Unlike the phoenix, I cannot transform my anguish into creative expressions of new life. The similarities between my experiences of creativity and the experiences of physical death described in recent literature are striking.[14] Liberation (resurrection), in both cases, demands the experience of nothingness.

To reach liberation, the *Tibetan Book of the Dead* says that we must abandon all fears regarding death. We must abandon our dualistic way of perceiving death as opposed to life.[15] We must passion-ately believe in the ultimate oneness of life and death; we must wholeheartedly embrace nothingness and recognize therein the unity of all opposites. The Gospel stories of the Samaritan woman at the well, the dialogue of Jesus with Nicodemus, and the curing of the blind man all affirm this. "No one who believes will be condemned; but whoever refuses to believe is condemned already" (Jn. 3:18). "If you believe, even though you die, you will live, and whoever lives and believes will never die" (Jn. 11:26). Only after they believe—in something or someone else or in their own goodness—can the characters in these three stories move toward nothingness and its resultant liberation.

To a certain extent, believing is a passion we choose. Beyond that, the ability to believe is a gift which is either given or not given to us. Sometimes we can get so immersed in existential anxiety that we cannot believe in anything. Then we are much like the dead Lazarus who is cut off from others and incapable of helping himself. But even this situation is not without hope. As the Gospels and the *Tibetan Book of the Dead* attest, the passion of others can set us free when we cannot liberate ourselves. The persistent love of Martha and Mary moves Jesus to help Lazarus. The belief and prayers of these two women help Lazarus experience resurrection.

Resurrection, a sacrament like baptism, happens continually throughout life. It is an experience that takes place every time I discern honestly who I am and where I am going. It happens every time someone loves me and leads me forward beyond my own confinements. I experience new life whenever someone cares enough to believe in me: not the me that fits into a certain structure, but the whole of me, with all my assets and defects. Real love always means death, always means pain. But the pain is always a summons to grow. When passion is there, I can go forward through suffering, simply because I must respond. Love makes me keep going through the flames of self-knowledge. Like the mythical phoenix, I can then burst through my boundaries. By entering into nothingness, I in turn can become a giver of life. Because I have been touched and freed myself, I can then freely touch others.

❧ 4. MIDNIGHT SUN

THE discernment of nothingness is crucial to celibate passion. Such discernment, however, immediately poses other questions. Why do we find it so hard to leave behind our usual reactions to anxiety? Why is it we so often lack courage, have little faith, or stifle the passion of love? Why are we content to live in the lowlands and valleys and never approach the mountain of wholeness? Why do we settle for answers that are not answers and lives that are not alive? For me, these questions relate directly to the quality of my prayer.

The Second Vatican Council rightly indicated that prayer is part of being human. Thus it is an activity which belongs to all of us. If we are striving to be human, no rules should be needed to induce us to pray. Our entire being should be on fire, blazing with the intensity of the divine presence. But this is not how I have felt very often in prayer, nor is it the usual experience of many of my friends who pray. Instead of an overpowering burst of new freedom, souls afire with a deep consuming communion with God, many of us have felt like cold, dying embers. Our desire to pray is certainly there, as evidenced by our increased participation in Ignatian thirty-day retreats, yoga or transcendental meditation classes, Silva mind control or altered states of consciousness workshops, charismatic or other types of prayer groups. But something important appears to be missing. We seem to be no closer to God after these experiences than we were before.

I think the reason for our frustration with prayer is that few of us, in or out of convents and monasteries, understand what prayer is. Our expectations of prayer are usually one-sided. We think that in prayer we should feel good inside, at peace with ourselves and with the world around us. If we pray well, we believe God will reward us with his consolations. If we behave ourselves, we will merit his attention and we will gradually become perfect. When, instead, we experience prolonged periods of aridity and no favoritism from God, we believe we have failed. When we experience nothing at all in prayer, we begin to suspect that God is not there. When we see no improvement in our personal quirks and eccentricities, our limitations and ego-centeredness, we may give up altogether. Thus, with no one to guide us, we settle for less, or perhaps for no, prayer at all.

It seems to me that we must expect prayer to have as many tensions as does our physical life. A certain amount of stress, physiologists tell us, is actually good for us. It causes our blood to flow, our lungs to expand, and our muscles to contract. As physicists explain to us, there always exists a tension or friction between two related objects. The closer these objects come to each other, the greater the stress, the greater the forces of attraction and repulsion. How can we expect anything different from our prayer life? Because prayer is an evolving relationship between two beings, there must be continual tension. There will be times when the stress is minimal and we experience peace; but there will also be times when the stress becomes nightmarish and the pain, gargantuan.

When I experience heightened stress, darkness, or aridity in prayer, I often panic. I think I have done something wrong. Having studied how the body responds to stress, I have come to believe that stress in prayer is something normal, something we must learn to deal with. How we respond is extremely important. On the physical level, a failure to adapt to stress may lead to early death.

So too, how we respond to aridity and darkness in prayer may lead us to spiritual ecstasy or spiritual death.

Life always implies friction between opposites. Uniformity is death. Sometimes prayer is warm and consoling, filled with light as from a candle. But sometimes it is cold and despairing, filled with darkness like a charred forest after a huge brush fire. Down through the centuries, mystics have defined their spiritualities according to these opposites. Some theologians, Origen, St. Augustine, St. Bernard, St. Thomas Aquinas, have fostered the concept of prayer as an ever-increasing dimension of light. Others, such as St. Gregory of Nyssa, Dionysius the Areopagite, and St. John of the Cross, have written of prayer's predominant darkness. I think one mistake we have made is to regard prayer as solely light or solely darkness. We have forgotten that desolation and aridity are normal occurrences which are part of a growing human-divine relationship.

Prayer is a burning. If the fire inside us is great, it will burn regardless of the dirt or the water we throw upon it. If that flame is small, the smallest breeze will blow it out. So it is with these times of light and darkness. If we continue to spend ourselves in fragmented pursuits and superficial prayer, we will not have enough energy to last us through the night. Cold, frightened, and without fuel to light the way, we will either fall asleep in the hour of agony, as did the apostles (see Mt. 26:40), or we will be doomed to continue our wanderings, as did the five foolish virgins (see Mt. 25:1–13).

Matthew's account of the wise and foolish virgins tells me that prayer has everything to do with celibate passion. To pray is to be celibate and to be passionate. It is to remain faithful to vigilancy, watchfulness, waiting. It is to be passionately involved in the same love affair all night long. It is to keep the home fires burning throughout the night, to wait for the dawn, and to believe that the sun will come again. Prayer is the celibate part of me which never sleeps. It is the "all-night virgin" within me which embraces the nights, perhaps a whole lifetime of nights, waiting for, watching with, and being in the company of the Beloved.

To understand prayer and to understand celibate passion, we must, I think, re-evaluate our conception of detachment and attachment. The detachment people feel in our technological world of crowds and numbers is not the same detachment required of celibate passion. The former experience is alienation rather than a real detachment. It is estrangement, loneliness, and despair. We "detach" ourselves from real situations and real people with intellectual rationalizations, philosophical truisms, and sometimes even "spiritual" discernment. We isolate ourselves from others in an effort to maintain our treasures, to build up our fortunes, or to "get closer to God." This, I feel, is what happens when we are only half celibate, alone but not vigilant. Like many of the commodities in our disposable society, we tend to discard people without ever having seen, known, appreciated, or loved them. It may take a fuel shortage, a bus strike, an ecological crisis, a sudden accident, or even a death to make us understand the significance of these things and these people. Only when it is too late do we sense the importance of the missing person or dog or article, only then do we value them for themselves.

Celibate passion is a revolutionary countercurrent to this type of detachment. This passion is so strong that none of the aridities or desolations in our prayer or in our physical life can dissuade us from our single quest. Celibate passion is a passion that is so rightly attached to all beings that everything in the world can be lifted up, transfigured, and consumed by the divine presence. To be celibate is to be wholeheartedly involved in the good times and to patiently ride out the bad times. It is to perceive the meaning of paradox and to appreciate the rhythmic quality of all life.

Such rhythms as talking and listening, initiative and receptivity, action and stillness, presence and absence, are necessary parts of any kind of communication. Spiritual directors are now realizing that what happens in our prayer life may be directly correlated to the rhythms in our physical life. In the oscillations of consolation and desolation there are distinct patterns which are sometimes based on our internal hormonal balance. But spiritual directors also realize that these oscillations do not originate solely from our chemistry. The Divine comes and goes. He is present and he is absent. "God opens up to us when he wants to reveal himself; he takes away his company when he sees fit to do so."[1] We cannot manipulate or control him. As C. S. Lewis describes:

> One day you'll see him and another you won't. He doesn't like being tied down—and of course he has other countries to attend to. It's quite all right. He'll often drop in. Only you mustn't press him. He's wild, you know.[2]

As there is a season for everything, so too is there a time of consolation in every stage of growth in our relationship with God. Some of these times are more intense than others. Some are marked with a prayerful quiet or a delectable absorption without pain. Sometimes they are joyous exaltations which inebriate us. They are flashes of light, filled with expansive sensations and euphoric awareness. Sometimes a sense of God's company overwhelms us. We feel that he is near and that he walks beside us. Such consolations are like rich treasures which delightfully absorb our attention.

I believe the purpose of these consolations is to detach us slowly and persistently from all that is not God. Because they fill us with his presence, we become aware of his greatness and grandeur, and we are led to a greater self-knowledge. The more we perceive of God, the greater grows our sorrow for sin. We are saddened by our ingratitude to the One who has given us so much. As Teresa of Avila writes:

> The greater the favor the soul receives, the less by far it esteems itself, the more keenly it remembers its sins, the more forgetful it is of its own interest, the more fervent are the efforts of its will and memory in seeking nothing but the honor of God.[3]

Little by little, we withdraw from temporary pleasures and egotistical pursuits to become more God-centered. As the psalmist says, "You changed my mourning into dancing; you took off my sackcloth and clothed me with gladness, that my soul might sing praise to you without ceasing" (Ps. 30:11–12). Eventually these consolations increase in intensity until we desire God and God only.

During times of consolation, prayer is a positive experience. We are flooded with illumination and enlightenment. We are carried into the abyss of divine light, Richard of St. Victor says. The mind "is surrounded on all sides by the fire of divine love; it is inwardly penetrated and inflamed."[4] This prayer is like white heat, and we ourselves become the flame. St. John of the Cross describes the soul in this state as a clear and pure crystal. St. Teresa says that in such moments we become like the sun, or like transparent diamonds, with a brilliance much greater than any we have ever experienced.

This type of communication demands our total involvement. For this reason, many systems of meditation outline methods for constant remembering, increasing awareness, and developing powers of concentration. We must spend time to listen and to receive. When God speaks, our souls melt (see Sg. 5:6), and we have no strength left to resist (see Lm. 1.13). The poet Kabir writes:

> Since the day when I met with my Lord,
>   there has been no end to the sport of our love . . .
> I see with eyes open and smile, and
>   behold his beauty everywhere.
> I utter his name, and whatever I see, it
>   reminds me of him; whatever I do,
>   it becomes his worship . . .
> Wherever I go, I move round him,
> All I achieve is his service:
> When I lie down, I lie prostrate
>   at his feet . . .
> Whether I rise or sit down, I can
>   never forget him; for the rhythm
>   of his music beats in my ears.[5]

God's fire evokes fire within us.

If prayer consisted only in such consolations, we would be tempted like the Thessalonians to stop living, or we would be tempted to pray for the good feelings it produced in us. We would too easily become attached to something that is not God, and wrongly detached from the world around us. Thus, perhaps it is better for us that each consolation has its corresponding moments of desolation, that the Ish of joy turns into the Esh of suffering.

Spiritual desolation, the mystics agree, is much more horrible than physical pain. When we pray during these times, it is like talking to someone who is not there at all. We feel that God has become a total stranger. As Meister Eckhart and St. Gertrude describe the experience, we feel that an impenetrable wall or thick hedge has come between us and God. The feelings of aloneness, forsakenness, and helplessness fill us with many yearnings. We are like ulcerated wounds, continually bleeding and burning with pain. According to St. Teresa, it is to know the torments of hell and to know no consolation.[6] John of the Cross confirms this comparison:

> What the sorrowful soul feels most in this condition is its clear perception, as it thinks, that God has abandoned it, and, in His abhorrence of it, has flung it into darkness; it is a grave and piteous grief for it to believe that God has forsaken it. . . . When this purgative contemplation is most severe, the soul feels very keenly the shadow of death and the pain of hell, which consist in its feeling itself to be without God, and chastised and cast out, and unworthy of him. . . . All this is felt by the soul in this condition, yes, and more, for it believes (with a fearful apprehension) that it is so with it forever.[7]

According to Evelyn Underhill, the desolation of God's absence can take one of two forms, depending upon the type of prayer we have experienced. For some, it is "the anguish of a lover who has lost the Beloved; in others, it is the intellectual darkness and confusion which overwhelms everything else."[8] Once we have known some of the exquisite moments of prayer, this feeling of loss can become intolerable. "Once in my security I said, 'I shall never be disturbed.' . . . You had endowed me with majesty and strength. But now when you hide your face, I am terrified" (Ps. 30:6–7). We are shocked by the silence; we try to deny what has happened; we complain, cry, and scream out for God's presence, only to realize with horror that he is not to be found.

This, to me, has been our contemporary experience of prayer. We have tried, like Daedalus, to fly too close to the sun, and our wings have melted away. Suddenly we have found ourselves falling into the cold waters of darkness. "You have plunged me to the bottom of the pit, to its darkest, deepest place, weighted down by your anger, drowned beneath your wave" (Ps. 88:6–7). Like Humpty Dumpty, it seems that no one can put us together again. All of our conceptions and beliefs which once reached the heights, now crumble in a babel of confusion. Instead of happiness, there is sorrow. Instead of light, we find only darkness (see Jb. 30:26). Drowned in the experience of Esh, we yearn even more ardently for the pentecostal fires which can weld together our broken parts.

My own times of desolation in prayer have brought me to parts of Scripture I had previously overlooked. I find in the ancient Hebrew poets companions to share my misery. "Yahweh, my soul is troubled. . . . I am bereft of strength: alone, among those you have forgotten, deprived of your protecting hand" (Ps. 88:3–5). "As a doe longs for running streams, so my soul longs for you. My soul thirsts for you, my life. When shall I go and see you? I have no food but tears day and night. I remember you and my soul melts within me" (Ps. 42:1–4). "Why do you reject me? Why do you hide your face from me?" (Ps. 88:14). "On my bed at night, I seek you whom my heart loves. I seek but do not find you" (Sg. 3:2).

The atheistic existentialists would have us believe that God is not really there. But the Zen masters tell us it is in darkness that we come closest to true vision. *Satori* is not an enlightenment but an extinguishing. To become desolate is to enter into divine union. Other mystics agree that God is present to us in these times of darkness. So near that, like St. Paul, we are blinded by the excess light. The desolations are necessary, some writers on the spiritual life stress, in order to experience greater consolations. The night-mares of midnight will turn into the ecstasy of dawn. "At night-fall, weeping enters in, but with the dawn, rejoicing" (Ps. 30:5). Rabindranath Tagore confirms this belief, "I bring to thee, night, my day's empty cup, to be cleansed with thy cool darkness for a new morning's festival."9 Darkness is only a preparation and a drying out so that the soul, like dry kindling, may burst into flame at its first contact with the divine Ish.[10]

St. John of the Cross delineates three major fluctuations of consolation and desolation in the soul's journey toward God. He calls each of these stages a "dark night."[11] The first night, that of the senses, is analogous to the darkness we experience at sunset. During twilight, our senses become darkened. We have trouble seeing. The oscillating rhythms of this night are like the ebb and flow of the ocean's tide. Constantly, God flows over us and then retreats. We sense his magnificent initiative, and we taste his salty waters. When he leaves, we wildly thirst for more. With the incoming tide, we bask lavishly in his presence, delighting in his company, not so much because of who he is but because his attention satisfies our needs and increases our self-esteem.

In this first consolation we tend to worship ourselves instead of God. We may reject the physical world and give up sensory attachments because our experience of prayer provides us with more satisfying pleasures. In this stage of our journey we have simply replaced our psychological or physical addictions with new ones. Thus, when we reach the first long stretch of aridity, we are thrown into crisis. Many of us fall down here. We realize we are still not happy; instead of praying, we have been seeking ourselves. Although spiritual directors maintain that this darkness is a necessary period of washing, cleansing, and self-emptying, many of us abandon the journey here. We are willing to throw away things which don't mean that much to us, but cannot quite muster the determination to relinquish costly things.

I think it is because we stop here that so many of us end up living lives of perpetual compromise. We are Christians in name only. We dilute the dreams we once had, the fervor that once burned inside us, the values we once prized. We settle for less because we are not willing to suffer. We tend to compensate for our innate emptiness by drowning ourselves in food, alcohol, sex, or possessions. We deny that, at our core, we are celibate; we forget that we have a destiny.

We cannot reach the second night of prayer unless we have faithfully suffered through the first one. This new darkness, which

John of the Cross compares to the midnight hours, may not occur until after many years. Here, the rhythms of God's presence and absence are more dynamic than during the first night. These periods last longer and are more consistent, like the rhythm of low and high tides throughout the day. At high tide, the soul is bathed continually in the ecstasy of God's nearness. But as low tide nears, we are left even longer alone on the shore. Because this period of darkness is more terrible and lengthy than anything previously experienced, medium-souled persons now turn back.

Here in this second dark night we realize that we often worship our concepts of God rather than God himself. We come to acknowledge that we haven't really seen or heard or touched him. We have detached ourselves, but we have kept him at a distance by building philosophical or theological cages around him or by trying to dictate our wills to him. We have tried to fit him into our plans and our lives, and have forgotten to approach him as personal, as a God more human, more whole, than we could ever become in this world, more sensitive and responsive in suffering than anyone else in creation. We have not understood that we need to attach ourselves to his ever-generous love and concern.

The last night which John of the Cross describes is experienced by only a very few persons. This is so, not because only a few are called to this level of prayer, but because few are persistent enough to stay awake the whole night. Few of us have enjoyed God enough to suffer this last desolation. St. John describes this prayer as the darkest darkness and the coldest hour of the night, occurring just before dawn. The rhythms of this night are the most violent and devastating of all. This is what John calls "the night of God," a night in which we realize that we have attached ourselves to his personal presence and, in so doing, have limited and reduced God to our own defined circumference of faith. In this night, we must learn to attach ourselves purely and singleheartedly to nothing, not even to God. In this night, we come naked before the God of all possibilities, all powers, and all dimensions. He is the God beyond our capacity, beyond our comprehension, beyond our grasp. We must somehow leap, not even into the Abyss, but beyond it, with a courage and heroism that only long-term saints (or lunatics) can muster.

This dark night is a last pruning period of aridity and desolation, a tremendous upheaval in the process of "unselfing." We are stimulated to new growth. We can no longer rely on our own resources; we must totally surrender to the pruner. This surrender, far from being masochistic, as psychiatrists like Freud would imagine it, is the highest idealization and achievement we can attain.[12] Our last elements of spiritual coarseness and vulgarity are blasted away. Our imperfections are "roused from their sleep, purged of illusion, and forced to join the growing stream."[13]

St. Bernard defines this stream of growth as a maturing development of love. In the early stages of prayer, the self loves only itself. In the second degree of love, we love God because we need him to make up for our own inadequacies. The third type of love is a love for God, but for his consolations and goodness. The highest form of love, however, is love of God for his sake only. It is the transition between the third and fourth stages of love and then beyond these loves that I believe John of the Cross describes in his last most terrifying night. Here, I think we learn the very secret of sanctity: "to renounce not only everything earthly, but also everything Divine."[14]

As long as we desire anything, even if it is God, we are not purely pursuing one thing; we are not loving one thing alone. The purpose of the dark nights is to wean us away from our spiritual pabulum and from our childish satisfactions (see 1 Co. 3:1–2). We must not only refuse to be satisfied with less than God, we must not seek to be satisfied with anything at all. Thomas Merton strongly agrees with this.

> Only when we are able to "let go" of everything within us, all desire to see, to know, to taste, and to experience the presence of God, do we truly become able to experience that presence with the overwhelming conviction and reality that revolutionize our entire inner life.[15]

Real prayer takes us beyond faith. Deprived of the light for clear vision, we must continue blindly. Leaving behind everything, we must, like flying fish, leap out of the water and "enter a more ethereal atmosphere that is filled with madness."[16] As Jesus on the road to Calvary falls three times and then continues, so must we push on through these three nights and keep journeying toward the dawn. We must embrace the absurd and go beyond everything we have ever known.

Although it may seem eternal, the last night of John of the Cross will eventually break. But for most of us, the suffering breaks us first. Only a very few strong-souled individuals will see the morning's dawn before their death. They are the genuine celibates whose passion drives them ceaselessly through the dark nights to the bridal chamber. There, the increased tension between the human and the divine will reach the highest possible intensity before indissoluble oneness. Passion will erupt as in the orgasmic rhythm of lovers, pulsing to the same ecstatic delights and ending in blissful union. God's eternal phallic battering ram will at last break through our egotistical barriers. The human will transcend all possible attachments, to become open and free, relaxed and expansive, allowing the full deluge of God's passion to explode in the soul's innermost caverns, filling, flooding, and saturating it with new life.

To arrive at the bridal chamber, there can be no short cuts. We cannot approach prayer as we do everything else in our push-button, instant society. There are no prayer pills or enlightenment capsules. Any relationship worth developing requires a tremendous amount of darkness and suffering. As John Tauler reminds us, God will not always be there to caress and enkindle us. Rather, we must rouse ourselves in this journey toward him. Only in the greatest darkness and in the most anguished suffering are we closest to our final break-through. It is here that "we stand, suddenly at the confines of human thought, and far beyond the Polar circle of the mind . . . and the midnight sun reigns over that rolling sea where the psychology of man mingles with the psychology of God."[17]

✿ 5. BURNING GROUND

THE word *God* has appeared many times in the first four chapters of this book, but I have written almost nothing about who I perceive God to be. An impossible task, perhaps. How can I dare even attempt to describe him? I can't, and yet I must. I believe that to be human, to be religious, and to pray, is necessarily related to my comprehension of who God is. Without firsthand experience of him, celibate passion is artificial, absurd, and meaningless. But where can I begin and what shall I say? Perhaps this: I am one who prays and I know beyond a doubt that I am answered.

Beyond that, I hesitate. For God is too much for me, much more than I could ever grasp or contain or understand. Just when I think I know him, he surprises me by a new revelation. He pulls out a new face from his bag of tricks. Once again I am startled and thrown into confusion. I don't know if it is because these are complicated times or because my own psyche is complicated that I find God so complex. Sometimes I am a monist, for I experience him as a nebulous force outside me; sometimes I am a monotheist, experiencing God as personal, present, and caring. There are times when he seems to be so many different and contrary things that I can almost call myself a polytheist or pantheist. And there are even times when I am so deprived of his presence that I feel like an atheist.

I have read enough about heretics to fear that I too am risking censure. No doubt, my current conceptions will be tempered by more living. But I cannot overlook the experiences I have had, nor can I ignore the ways God as come to me. It seems that whenever he reveals himself, it must always be in bits and pieces because our capacities are so limited. Thus, what we write will always be based on only partial understanding and will always be to some extent heretical.

The Old Testament has been a tremendous support for me in my struggle to discern and make sense out of who God is. I find in the ancient Hebrew writers my own questions, the same experiences and sense of contradictions. God is indeed a mystery. He is not one thing to the exclusion of another. He is both Ish and Esh, active and passive, masculine and feminine, good and evil, just and merciful. These concepts are not mere theological speculations about his attributes. They are expressions of the Hebrews' experience. God is simultaneously the God of fire who spews out smoke and live embers (see Ps. 18:6–8), and the God of earth who nourishes all creatures and renews their life (see Ps. 104:28,30).

We Westerners seem to have a propensity for "either/or" logic. For centuries, we one-sidedly perceived God as fire. He was an active God, good, warm, and protecting. He was the reward giver and the God of justice. His wrath would certainly descend upon the disobedient and sinful. My own childhood was filled with moments of terror and guilt, stemming from what I now consider to be the heresy of puritanism. Hell-fire and damnation grew to demonic proportions in my mind, and the road to salvation became much too straight and narrow. To respond to this type of God was to view the world as antagonistic to the ideal of perfection. I remember being taught, and for many years believing, that a religious vocation was better than the vocation to marriage, and that contemplation was "higher" or "more perfect" than apostolic activity.

In the ten years preceding Vatican II, our conception of God began to shift. Slowly, we have been presented with the God of earth. This is the God who is in the mountains and lakes, the city, the university, the movie studio, and in each person. He is the God of secularism, naturalism, and rationalism. He is loving and faithful, and although we continue to speak of him in masculine terms, he has become the Divine Mother. No sin or evil is too great to separate us forever from his love. God now seems somewhat passive. Correspondingly, today's religious person is defined as someone extremely involved and active. The tide of opinion has swung so dramatically toward activism that the contemplative life is perceived by some as a selfish refusal to spend oneself. Contemplation is now seen as less desirable than apostolic activity. Religious vows are not holier than marriage vows.

I find myself reacting to the God of our contemporary theologies. This one-dimensional God is not the God I experience. For me, God has both good and bad characteristics. As fire, he has been both loving and dangerous; as earth, he has been both supportive and evil. He builds me up and he breaks me down. He gives me life and he destroys me. He consoles me and leads me to the pit of desolation.

My first experience of God, which happened when I was eighteen months old, was that of a positive, warm energy which surrounded and protected me. God was a presence, a power which I believed would take care of me. Several times since then this same God has revisited me. Sometimes he has been a blazing fire which ravishes and consumes me. Sometimes he has been a brilliant light, a power of warmth and happiness. He bestows life upon me, affirming and consecrating me with his gentle love. He is there and he speaks clearly.

It is no small wonder to me that the Bible is filled with examples of this God of fire. He is the burning bush which appears to Moses (Ex. 3:2), the pillar of light which accompanies the Israelites on their flight from Egypt (Ex. 13:21–22), the devouring fire which burns on Mount Sinai (Ex. 19:18; 24:17). He is the ever-present God of goodness. In him, there is no darkness (Ps. 139:9–10). He is a light which darkness cannot overpower. The God of Jesus is the same God of Moses on Sinai and of Elijah on Horeb. On the mountain of transfiguration, Jesus prays and the features of his face become as brilliant as lightning (Lk. 9:29–30). An encounter with the risen Jesus produces the same effects in his apostles on their way to Emmaus. "Did not our hearts burn within us as he talked to us on the road and explained the scriptures to us?" (Lk. 24:32).

Throughout my childhood, this God of fire overwhelmed me with his grandeur and his greatness. I was fascinated by the ways he came. Sometimes his presence so overcame me that he seemed more real than my parents or my baby brother. What seems so striking about this God is that I never was afraid when he came. I simply trusted, and he never disappointed me. I spent hours of every day talking with him and sharing both my sorrows and my joys. He was my faithful companion, and all I needed to do to find him was to return to my innermost self. As I grew older he became a vehement lover whose passion pursued and captured me over and over again.

Monism or monotheism? I cannot say, for these experiences of God have been sometimes one and sometimes the other. Sometimes, as described by John Ruysbroek, a Flemish mystic of the fourteenth century, God has been for me a light "blazing down as it were a lightning flash . . . bringing so great a joy and delight of soul and body"[1] that I am totally astounded. He is an inner light, the same infinite ocean of love George Fox wrote about. Like the God of St. Augustine, he is a light that breaks through my darkness.[2] He flashes, shines, and chases away my blindness. Personal and yet impersonal, this light burns with an indescribable luster, warming me and enkindling love. He is my meaning and my reason for living.

My experiences of the God of fire gradually changed from positive to negative. Like a child who gets burned when touching an entrancing flame, I learned to fear this God. He was no longer for me simply a fire that was breathtaking to behold; he was the fire that could also sear, scorch, and destroy me. He was a mysterious power of unlimited capacities over which I had no control. I learned to respect this God, to revere him as sacred, and to approach him very carefully. I could not be careless. He was the initiator, the controller; he was capable of wrath, anger, and jealousy. He demanded obedience to his precepts, and when I was unfaithful, he punished me with the full blast of his fiery furnace.

At first I thought that anger, hatred, and violence were human characteristics we ascribed to God. When I encountered these emotions as a child, I often ran to God for comfort and protection. But then came a day when he did not comfort me, and instead lashed out in fury. I was shocked and horrified. It was difficult to believe that God could really be like that. Sometimes I still have a hard time believing it. But every time I am not true to him, his anger blazes out at me.

Perhaps if I had not thought that scriptural references to God's wrath were just superstitious beliefs, I would have been more prepared to meet this God. Whenever the Israelites lose faith in God and no longer trust in his power to save them, we are told that God is angered (see Ps. 78:21). His is rage that will burn forever, says the prophet Jeremiah. "I will enslave you to your enemies in a country which you do not know, for my anger has kindled a fire that will burn you up" (Jr. 15:14). "Yes, a fire has blazed from my anger; it will burn to the depths of Sheol. It will devour the earth and all its produce; it will set fire to the foundations of the mountain" (Dt. 32:22). Not only does God's wrath descend upon our public sins but, as I found out only too well, he probes our hearts and knows our innermost infidelities. "We are burnt up by your anger and terrified by your fury; . . . you inspect our secrets by your own light" (Ps. 90:7–8).

There were two results of this experience of God's anger as a child. First, I tried even harder to be perfect and to merit God's love. And second, I called on him to avenge me whenever I was wronged. In my childhood I was sometimes a minature Joan of Arc, using the weapons of war and prayer to demolish my enemies. "My God, bowl (them) along like tumbleweed, like chaff at the mercy of the wind; as fire devours the forest, as the flame licks up the mountain" (Ps. 83:13). "May red-hot embers rain down upon my enemies" (Ps. 140:10). As I grew, I discovered that my enemies still thrived, while I continued to suffer. Even when I was good, I was still in pain, and my environment did not change. I was afraid because this new revelation of God did not make sense to me. God was no longer the intensely burning flame; he was a silent candle flickering within me, a pain which slowly ate away at me. Gradually, I realized that my God had become the disciplinarian. As fire was used in traditional Hebrew sacrifices to cleanse the unholy, so too was God refining me.

Many times during my life I have known God to be a strict taskmaster. In these moments, he is someone I trust and consider good. I believe he loves me, and because he wants to love me even more, he is fashioning me (somewhat as Pygmalion did Galatea) into a woman worthy of his love. To reach him, I must walk through the fire and believe he will not let me perish (refer to Is. 43:2). The God who has been inside me is now outside. As Dr. D. T. Suzuki notes, to obtain him is no easy task. "It is a kind of fiery baptism, and one has to go through the storm, the earthquake, the overthrowing of the mountains and the breaking in pieces of the rocks."³ God is a consuming fire, and although I can hardly bear the agony, I am continually drawn closer to him, as a moth is drawn toward a light. He brands me with hot coals, and I must submit. He purifies me, and I must undergo the ordeal.

For me, God has definitely been a jealous God. Sometimes I feel that he burns with jealousy for me (Zc. 8:2) and that he wants to make sure he always has a place in my heart. There is a hollow inside me, a celibate space, reserved for him and him only. Even when he chooses to be distant, he will not let me fill that space with any other love. But when he fills that space, he takes me to himself as a bridegroom does his bride, transforming me into himself. During one of these times, I wrote the following in my journal:

> Perhaps the world would call me poor because I am celibate. But never in my life have I felt richer. For I'm wedded to a kingdom and a king who loves me. There are those who would think me hungry, yearning for someone with whom to spend the night. But I have never feasted so lavishly or drunk so voluptuously. Although hungry, I am con-

stantly fed. Some people in the world think I cry from loneliness, but all I can do is laugh. For I am never alone, and sometimes when I weep, it is from joy.

Ah, yes, I am poor, impoverished in my limitations and weaknesses. Yes, I am hungry, for I never seem to get enough of you to be too long satisfied. And yes, I cry often, to think I have so far yet to go on the road to perfection. But perhaps this is why you have been so good to me . . . for I really need you.

Earth cannot meet fire and remain unchanged. Neither have I been able to experience God's presence and remain unscorched. I surrender to his passion. I am salted with his fire; I cannot remain lukewarm. He has touched me and, like St. Augustine, I burn for his embrace.

The message and ministry of Jesus not only present God as fire, but simultaneously as earth. Although this second God has been as much a part of the Hebrew tradition as the former, she had receded into the background and been temporarily forgotten. The God of earth is a God who resides in nature and within each person. This God is the divine feminine, who supports but is passive, who is fruitful but dark and mysterious. This God is a mother who nurses her children back to health [compare the Gospel accounts of the cure of Simon's mother-in-law (Mt. 8:14–15), the raising of the official's daughter (Mk. 5:21–24), and the cure of the woman with the hemorrhage (Lk. 8:43–48)]. This God is compassionate and merciful, rejoicing when we return home [compare the story of Mary Magdalen and the annointing of Jesus' feet (Lk. 7:36–50), and the parables of the lost sheep (Mt. 18:-12–14), the lost drachma (Lk. 15:8–10), and the prodigal son (Lk. 15:11–32)].

The God of earth has been the most difficult God for me to understand. I have always experienced her, but have not always acknowledged her. Because of her, I struggle with moments of pantheism and polytheism, with moments of agnosticism and atheism. She is the God I have found in the twinkle of a friend's eye, in the silly antics of a sheep dog named Zorba, in the dark forest floor of Muir Woods, in the Japanese garden of the Huntington Library, and in the midnight hours on Santa Monica beach. She is my relationship with each person and thing I love.

When I experience this earth-mother God, all things appear interconnected and personalized. I am enthralled and soothed by the God of nature, engrossed in the God of ecology. Love becomes an experience so intense that it shatters all my fears and inhibitions. It injects life into my blood, my bones, and my soul. I don't merely brush past life. I become steeped, surrounded, inundated. Life crashes through my defenses and leaves me spellbound.

I am not completely comfortable with this God, as I have said, perhaps because my original training separated the divine from the earthy. This is the God of sensuality, of flesh, of tangibility. This is the Hebrew God who has substance. She is not like the pagan gods who have "mouths but never speak, eyes but never see, ears but never hear, noses but never smell, hands but never touch, feet but never walk" (Ps. 115:5–7).

To know this God is not to limit her to a cerebral experience. This is the God I feel through every nerve fiber and blood vessel of my body. Like the ancient Hebrew who found God in manna, bread, wine, and oil, I can at times actually taste her. Sometimes she is sweet, sweeter than the chocolate of Ghirardelli Square, the ice cream of Clancy Muldoon, or the natural honey that comes straight from the comb (see Ezk. 3:3; Ps. 119:103). "O taste and see how good God is!" (Ps. 34:8). I sense her then in a new way. Instead of hearing her words, I devour them (see Ps. 19:10, Jr. 15:16). She becomes the fresh strawberry and the juicy medium-rare steak. Like the God of both the Old and New Testaments, she is someone I can eat and drink (refer to Si. 24:21; Mt. 5:6; Jn. 4:13–14).

Sometimes this God is so close I can smell her. She may have the pungent fishy smell of San Francisco's wharf, the tantalizing aroma of freshly baked bread and newly popped corn. She is the fragrance of a certain after-shave lotion and the odor of a country meadow. She "exhales a perfume like cinnamon and acacia;" she "breathes out a scent like choice myrrh, like galbanum, onycha, and stacte, like the smoke of incense in the tabernacle" (Si. 24:15). She is the crisp smell of a cold winter day and the moist fertile smell of a rich compost pile.

Of all my senses, the weakest is sight. Only after years of much concentration and experience in prayer, have I begun to "see" God. My experience in the woods of Nova Scotia did much to heighten my visual acuity. There, God suddenly leapt out at me. I wrote in my journal on a July day in 1974:

> Will I ever be able to see enough of you? Will I ever have eyes big enough? You are in each needle on the pine trees; you are in the tall strong trunks of the birches, in the hard earthy rocks, stones, and pebbles; you are in each flower, each lily pad, each cat, each dog, and especially, each person.

Since then I have seen God in many things: maples, ferns, mushrooms, sarsparilla, hemlock, turtles, snakes, lichen, and porcupines. She is the variegated green countryside, the orange hues of the dawning sun, and the fog during a midnight canoe ride. I see her in fireflies as well as in jellyfish, and in the Pacific tides which etch in the sand exciting Zen gardens of pebbles and sea shells. Like the psalmist, I am seeing God's goodness, now while I live (Ps. 27:13). Whenever I see the world, really see it, I see her (see Jn. 14:9).

This God is also someone I can hear. She is in the piano music of Nancy Fierro and in the songs of Dan Schutte. Sometimes her footsteps are so loud they wake me in the night. Her voice resounds within me in clear, distinct sentences. At other times, I hear her simply in the sounds of nature: the sound of water evaporating from a blade of grass; the whooping crack of a frozen lake as it makes new ice; the bloodcurdling howl of a pack of coyotes; the snap, crackle, and pop of a bowl of Rice Krispies; the droaning mating calls of summer bull frogs; and the love whispers of a friend holding me.

But perhaps what I have loved most about this sensuous God is that she is a God who can touch and be touched. Like the God of Jeremiah, Isaiah, and Ezekiel, this God holds out her hand to me. She annoints me with oil (see Ps. 45); she heals me and makes me whole. She rushes over me as a hurricane or brushes over me as a delightful breeze. She lets me lie down on her lush fields; she bathes and soothes me with her waters. She is the God who affirms me by being totally present to me. She is the reverential presence of people who are not afraid to be intimate with me, people like Pat Sullivan, Terry Sweeney, or Theresa Harpin. Each of them unique and precious, each allowing me to touch God in a special way.

The God of earth has been everything for me. *Tat tvam asi.* She is this, she is that. But like the God of fire, this God also has a negative side. *Neti, neti.* She is the God who cannot be contained in beauty alone or in any particular relationship. She is a sad God, a God of brokenness, misunderstanding and poverty. She is the God of the streets. I have found her face in the most unlikely places: in a San Francisco VD clinic, in the disheveled body of a friend's alcoholic father, in a psychotic war veteran who lived with his cat at the end of the Marina del Rey jetty. She is the God of loneliness and discord, of divorce and tragedy. She is a strange God, silent, still, and vague. She is, as the *Secret of the Golden Flower* states, "the god of utmost emptiness."[4] When I taste her, instead of sweetness, I find death. In my journal I once wrote:

> My heart is an existential scream; my soul is an outstretched beggar. Never have I felt so desecrated, so assaulted, so raped. I failed, and now the dreariness outside almost matches my inner dullness. Everything seems blah. I am a singular cry in the wilderness, a yearning which flames with the desire for union. Someday, perhaps, I shall get there, but for now my desert has become soggy. Help me get used to the rain. Help me find you in this wetness.

> The pain racks my bones, burns through my blood, and devastates my muscles. You are killing me, Lord. Before me looms Golgotha and its foreboding death sentence. You stand before me, pulling me; you stand behind me, pushing me forward. You surround me on all sides, keeping me from dodging away. . . . I am a bleeding open sore, a body of bruises. My soul cries out to you to stop, but you remain silent. "I protest against such violence, but there is no reply" (Jb. 19:7).

This God is not gentle with me. Her arrows pierce deep (Ps. 38:2), and she wrenches me from my former relationships. She is the God of dissension and broken hearts (see Lk. 12:49–52). With ruthlessness, she knocks down what she has built and tears up what she has planted (see Jr. 45:4). "Yahweh Sabbaoth says this: I am going to break this people and this city just as one breaks a potter's pot" (Jr. 19:10–11); it shall be "irretrievably shattered, smashed, . . . so that of the fragments not one shard remains big enough to carry a cinder from the hearth or scoop water from the cistern" (Is. 30:14). So overwhelming is this God, so irrational and contradictory, that I wonder if she is not evil.

I think Jesus knew this same earth God, and I think he too was broken apart by her. "You have turned my friends against me and made me repulsive to them" (Ps. 88:8). "Even my closest and most trusted friend, who shared my table, rebels against me" (Ps. 41:9; compare Jn. 13:21). Jesus, too, experiences the hurt and disillusionment, the fickleness of loves lost. Part of what is so terrible in this experience is that there are no answers. God remains silent and passive. As Job cries out: "If I go eastward, you are not there, or westward, still I cannot see you. If I seek you in the north, you are not to be found, invisible still when I turn south" (Jb. 23:8–9). God has suddenly become an illusion. We are filled with doubt. She is the God we do not know.

It has taken me twenty-five years to perceive this God. She is the experience of failure, exhaustion, rejection. She is a wounded God, who becomes threadbare when I do, frustrated when I am, and wearied when I can no longer keep going. Like Jesus, she weeps over a situation she cannot change (Lk. 19:41); she cries when one of her friends dies (Jn. 11:35). "Tears flood my eyes night and day," says the God of Jeremiah (14:17). "How often I have longed to gather you together, as a mother hen gathers her brood under her wings" (Lk. 13:34). This God is somehow helpless in taking away my pain. When I suffer, she suffers.

I must emphasize that my experience of the God of fire has been vastly different from the God of earth. When God is fire, he is active, masculine, judging, good, and disciplining. Correspondingly, I am passive; in prayer, I become the traditional female. I still my faculties; only when my will, understanding, and reason are quiet, does he enter me. When God is earth, she is passive, feminine, natural, relational, loving. In prayer to this God, I become more active, more masculine, more sensual and intellectual. I find her in my involvement with others.

It seems to me that what spiritual writers call "infused contemplation" cannot be strictly passive. Our souls cannot be all feminine. This concept not only limits us but limits God. We must be able to achieve union with God in all possible modes and manners of expression. It seems to me that because God is both fire and earth, Jesus prays both actively and passively. He prays not only in solitary, isolated places but in times of intense activity. He not only uses his feminine powers of intuition to touch God; he uses his cerebral capacities as well.

I cannot expect God to be always the same. He changes, and my prayer likewise changes. Each day is new; each moment brings new risks. I never know who God will be for me, and I am slowly coming to accept this fact. Perhaps I am unraveling a long hidden secret. Perhaps when I let God be whole, I will myself become whole—more alive, more human, and more in touch with all being. For this I pray:

> Come to me, oh great and terrible God, and let me come to you. Make your presence rest in me. Penetrate my anguish; saturate my emptiness; encompass my longing. Devastate my being; overwhelm me with your passion; drown me in your love, that what I know of me may become you and what I experience of you may become me, until we reach that moment when no longer will it be possible to distinguish between us. Hold me fast in your embrace. Let me stay with you longer than I dare imagine, closer than my very breath, and so much in love with you that all I want is you. Let me take you in my arms and feel the warmth of joy that burns and welds my being to yourself. Fire me and make me smooth. Shape my edges and sorted ways into your shape and substance, until I melt within your love and there become forever fused.

"Because Thou lovest the Burning-ground,
I have made a Burning-ground of my heart—
That Thou, Dark One, haunter of the Burning-ground,
Mayest dance Thy eternal dance."[5]

ॐ 6. IMPASSIONED PRESENCE

TO burn for and to be grounded in the reality of God is the most important thing we can do with our lives. But even this is not enough. Once we have caught fire and have found our deepest center, then we must call forth the birthing of God in others. We must be midwives of new life. Celibate passion demands that we do something creative with our relationship to God. To be fully human, we must share him with those around us.

This insight has been one of the traditional justifications for choosing a celibate or solitary life-style. Celibacy supposedly gives us more freedom to pursue a career or to give ourselves in creative service. But this is only partly true. Instead of freeing us for greater creativity, celibacy often becomes a synonym for addiction to work. How easily we drown our lives in too much verbiage and paperwork, and limit our relationships to the stimulation of one small part of the anatomy. We spend so much of our time reproducing the past or maintaining the status quo that we neglect to develop the multi-dimensional, psycho-physical-spiritual beings we are.

In the book of Genesis, when God directs Adam and Eve to be fruitful, multiply, and fill the earth, he is referring to more than biological reproduction. Our vocation, whether we are religious, single, or married, is to be cocreators with God, to fill the earth with unique and unrepeatable forms of life. To do this, we must awaken ourselves to new levels of consciousness and experience. Such awakenings, however, always require time. Thus, I find that implicit in the call to wholeness is the call to leisure.

I stress leisure (as opposed to work) because it implies attitudes which are essential to creativity. In the ancient creation stories and myths, divine creativity is never the same as work. Work is purposeful activity, a duty marked by drudgery, a mechanical reproduction of something already existing. Divine creativity, as presented in Genesis, is so leisurely that it seems to be play. God savors, applauds, and rejoices in creating unique and beautiful things. And he does this, as is stated in the books of Ecclesiasticus and Proverbs, only after eons and eons. Before the beginning of the created universe, there was neither activity nor rest. God alone was there. Alone, and yet not alone; one, and yet three. And there was leisure: an intense, intimate relationship of presence and reciprocity.

It is not difficult to understand why we have lost sight of the importance of leisure for creativity. Inherent in our Protestant Ethic is an emphasis on work, which has gradually evolved into its overvaluation and a very limited concept of what it means. The utilitarianism of Jeremy Bentham has persuaded us that our greatest motivation for work is pleasure, which can only be measured by the utility, or usefulness, of the work. We have learned to equate usefulness with happiness, and the amount of work we do with virtue. In today's society, we are measured by the job we hold and by how many luxuries of the culture we can purchase.

Utilitarianism has so saturated our religious concepts that it is almost impossible for us to be leisurely. Somewhere in our cerebral memory banks, we know that idle hands are potentially evil, and that we are slothful if we prefer to "be" instead of "do." To be good is to work hard and to work always. We suspect options that smack of a Bohemian pursuit of pleasure and we feel guilty when we aren't engaged in anything. To relieve ourselves of this guilt, we make leisure work-oriented and centered around the values of utility, progress, and production. Our leisure must have a purpose, even if it is merely to rejuvenate our minds and revitalize our bodies. Many of us are simply modern-day reincarnations of Sisyphus, a worker chained to his function, never pausing from fruitless toil and never reaping the rewards of labor.

Genuine leisure, to my mind, is something which should so involve and captivate us that we become renewed, refreshed, and reenergized. And this, it seems, only happens when the universe, or a person, or a book, or whatever, can become a "Thou," when we can enter into dialogue with that which is before us. It was not until I removed myself from twentieth-century American culture for a year that I realized how little we allow for this. We seem to want to be distracted instead of involved. We "put in time" by immersing ourselves in frantic putterings. We never really face ourselves and become more in tune with the world. "Recreation" often does not mean a re-creation of the individual, but an evasion of self, a refusal to become totally immersed and absorbed. And as a result, we never really do get recharged. We become more exhausted and more out of touch than we were when we stopped working.

In colonial times, leisure time centered around the church, where people got in touch with each other and with God. Today, many of us spend our leisure time around the television set. I don't know if it is fair to say that television is actually replacing liturgical services as leisure activity, but the similarities between the two forms of leisure suggest that they are direct competitors for our attention. One could easily, it seems, replace the other.

In both watching television and attending a liturgy, most of us allow ourselves to be bored and usually do nothing about it. With television, we allow ourselves to sit back and be entertained. We are not challenged; we enter into no dialogue with the characters on the screen; we cannot change (except by switching channels) the story that is unfolding before us. The plots are pretty much the same, and we can usually anticipate the last scene. The same things can be said of Sunday liturgies in some parishes. There is a priest or minister actor, a choir or solo performers, and a congregation audience. For the most part, the average person's role is passive. We do not affect what is happening before us. Our absence or presence does not change the "dialogue," the prayers, or the ritual.

Routine is much easier and safer than an energetic attempt to write a new television script or plan a creative liturgy. But to acquiesce and remain passive is, I believe, extremely dehumanizing. We are not cultivating our minds and souls; we are not taking initiative or responsibility for the quality of our leisure. If life seems moderately good, we are content with that. As Walter Kerr states, mediocrity "becomes an absolute: the standard must neither dip below a modestly acceptable norm nor aspire to rise above it. 'Pretty good' is at once the minimum quality we are willing to give eye and ear to—and the maximum."[1] As a result, we become dull, lifeless, and isolated people.

Several years ago, Dr. Mortimer Adler gave a series of lectures on "the good life," leisure, and education. Like many other philosophers and theologians, he argued that the purpose of liberal education is to prepare us for leisure and leisurely pursuits. Dr. Adler defined leisure as a type of work, one focused on the actual development of the capacities and talents of the individual. To a society so steeped in utilitarianism, perhaps it is necessary to speak of both professional and leisure "work." (Professional work is that which we must do whether we like it or not; leisure work is that which we like to do and want to do.) By defining both of these activities as work, both can be regarded as part of our duty to society, and part of our vocation as human beings.

My concern with Dr. Adler's conception of leisure is that we may be tempted to identify it solely in utilitarian terms. True leisure contradicts utilitarianism; it has no purpose other than itself. We do not choose leisure to become better persons or to contribute to civilization. In leisure, we lose our obsession with the pragmatic and simply pursue the "good life" for its own sake. We learn to appreciate beauty as beauty and friendship for itself. We learn the meaning of love, self-esteem, and creative giving.

We can only become human, I am convinced, by taking time for leisure and by acquiring the attitudes of leisure. The call to be a whole person is a call to leisure in all of its most self-actualizing expressions. Aristotle, in *Politics*, says that leisure is so important that it is the center about which everything revolves. When we become more creative and playful, we become more like God. As Robert Neale says, "the maturation of the individual presents the opportunity of growing from playlessness to full play and . . . full play in the adult is religion."[2] "Full play," which "uses all the potentials offered at the particular developmental stages of the individual's physical, psychological, and social growth,"[3] is the same as Adler's "leisure work" or Maslow's "self-actualization." And this type of play is always an experience of the "holy,"[4] which results in wisdom.

Ironically enough, when we experience the "holy," the wisdom we perceive often seems more like foolishness (1 Cor. 1:27). Leisure leads us to a wisdom which seems crazy. It is this madness which characterizes King David as he dances before the Ark of the Covenant and St. Paul, who becomes a fool for Christ. True leisure in relationship to the holy produces what the Greeks call *eutrapelia*, a nimbleness of mind which enables us to play. It is a wise balance between too much laughter and too much seriousness. The seventh day of creation, then, is not a rest after a week of hard work; it is a festive celebration of new life and love. It is a time of uselessness, a time "where the goal is not to have but to be, not to own but to give, not to control but to share, not to subdue but to be in accord."[5]

Usually, the only time we really play is when we are children. This is why I find it significant that several ancient religions have myths of infant gods who create from their play. Dionysius, Hermes, Apollo, and Heracles are all world-creating children. The Christian savior is the child of Bethlehem. Children seem to know what leisure is. A child enters readily into the spirit of play, imagination, and creativity. A child can waste time and love every minute of it. A child can see things for the first time and can be delighted with beauty. Children express wholeness, Carl Jung tells us, because they do not get lost in the one-sidedness of adulthood. A child is thus a "symbol of the union of opposites: a mediator, bringer of healing . . . one who makes whole."[6] Perhaps this is why

Jesus insists that we must become like children to enter the kingdom of God.

We know very little about the childhood of Jesus. But we can get clues of what it was like from Luke's report that "the child Jesus grew in wisdom and grace" (Lk. 2:40, 52). Luke could have told us that Jesus grew in carpentry skills, but instead he uses *wisdom* and *grace,* two words associated with leisure. During his thirty years I think Jesus came to realize that, to be a person of God, one must take time to really see, to marvel at the mystery of being, and to penetrate to the essence of things. It is only by being there, in the presence of God, that one can grow in wisdom, discernment, and vision.

The Gospel tells us that when Jesus calls the apostles they leave behind their work to follow him (see Mk. 1:16–21). We could hardly say that the apostles never work from that day onward. What I think is meant is that when they come to know Jesus, their attitudes change. They leave behind their pragmatic, workaday attitudes and learn from him to be still, to suffer with others, and to appreciate the small things in life. Jesus teaches them to see the birds of the air, the lilies of the field, the widow with her mite, and the little children at their feet. He teaches them to think creatively, to expand their thoughts beyond traditional logic. God, he tells them, is everywhere and in everyone: the saint as well as the sinner, the Samaritan as well as the Jew, the woman as well as the man. And he teaches them prayer, not that of rote memory or constant petition, but that of simply being in the presence of God in silent adoration.

I have often wondered why Jesus refers to himself as a shepherd. He never tended sheep; instead, he was a carpenter. In the context of leisure, his identification as shepherd becomes understandable. The carpenter symbol has always been equated with hard work, usefulness, efficiency, productivity, and common sense. All good qualities, but qualities that can easily become lost in attitudes of pragmatism. The shepherd symbol, however, has always denoted a person of vision, someone who knows wisdom and leisure.

The shepherd symbolizes the responsible adult who has recap-

tured the essence of childhood. He or she embodies a sense of the
ineffable, an awareness of the grandeur of creation, a radical
amazement at all of reality. In various myths, the shepherd sees
the sacred in the ordinary and thus is the first to discover the
abandoned prince or the newly born offspring of the gods. It is
certainly not strange that a group of shepherds first discern the
signs of Jesus' birth. Nor is it strange that so many leaders of God's
people, Abel, Abraham, Joseph, Moses, and David, are also shepherds. Leisure produces the vision necessary for good shepherding
and wise leadership.

In taking time to stop and be still for awhile, to forget our
thoughts and plans, to listen to the sounds of the universe within
and around us, we reach new levels of awareness. Our minds are
suddenly absorbed by the beauty of particulars, whether immense
or infinitesimal. Common things which once seemed boring now
loom before us as exquisite works of art, capturing our interest and
engaging our curiosity. The frying pan we are washing suddenly
becomes sculpture; the rose in the garden becomes like no other
flower we have ever seen. Uniqueness intoxicates us; we yearn to
discover more of the mysteries that surround us. In each particular
we contemplate the universal. The world seems more profound,
more all-embracing, and more wondrous than we have ever before
realized. We are awed by a deepened sense that being itself is
something penetrable and comprehensible, but at the same time
unfathomable, everflowing, and inexhaustible.

I have found that the contemplative awareness found in leisure
may remain on a purely natural level, or it may soar to the heights
of religious experience. This awareness ushers us simultaneously
into our full human potentialities and into the silent ever-loving
presence of God. For this reason, the ancient Greeks considered
the contemplative life as the highest form of existence. In contemplation we become most like God the creator and the lover, and
thus, as Aristotle believed, achieve perfect happiness. This contemplation is not an intricately contrived state of altered consciousness, but the "relaxed and useless, focused attention of the
whole mind on reality, a simple intuitive gaze born of wonder and
love."[7]

In leisure, we learn with T. S. Eliot to regain our childlike eyes and "to know the place for the first time."[8] We look and we reverence. We are delighted once again and rejoice continuously in new loves and new adventures. We give recklessly of our undivided attention and once again "resume our childhood love affair with single, concrete objects: with one coffee table, with one back yard, with one human face."[9] We learn to love with no purpose; to face life without manipulation or exploitation. With no expectation whatsoever, we come, we are silent, and we take a long, long look. Our prayer ceases to be an obligation or duty. God and the soul "have fruition of each other in the deepest silence."[10] God becomes the heart of our being, the center of our lives, the priority of our day. We take time and make time, perhaps consciously at first, but then unconsciously, until at last we realize this is the way it must always be.

The wisdom of leisure is the knowledge of firsthand experience: a *sapientia* of communion, a tasting of the right things. More than a contemplation of the beautiful, it is a vital union which obliterates all barriers and joins the lover and beloved as one. It is an experienced knowledge in which the separateness of the ego begins to fade, and we enter rapturously into the object we are contemplating. Such union leads to a new creation on both the natural and the religious levels (see 2 Co. 5:17). So absorbing is this experience that we often lose our sense of time. Everything, past, present, and future, becomes here and now. Slowly, we learn to live wholly in each moment. As Zorba the Greek explains to his boss:

> I've stopped thinking all the time of what happened yesterday. And stopped asking myself what's going to happen tomorrow. What's happening today, this minute? That's what I care about. I say: What are you doing at this moment, Zorba? "I'm sleeping." Well, sleep well. What are you doing at this moment, Zorba? "I'm working." Well, work well. What are you doing at this moment, Zorba? "I'm kissing a woman." Well, kiss her well, Zorba, and forget all the rest while you're doing it; there's nothing else, only you and her.[11]

Everything, in this frame of mind, is a gift to be celebrated. We are inundated with new zest for life. We are so joyfully caught up in the moment that we learn more and more the ability of being present. Zorba's philosophy has become our own, and everything is thus made holy.

Living in the present moment teaches us a certain dependency and trust. There is more to life than what we put into it; the future is not always determined by our own efforts or plans. One of the saddest consequences of the growth of technology is that to a great extent we are no longer dependent on the seasons and the sun, the amount of rainfall or the fertility of the soil. No longer are we forced by nature to wait until the right time of growth or maturation.

It was not until I went to Nova Scotia that I made time in my life for nature. Living in those woods taught me to look, to wait, and to trust. The garden was not just a garden, but a miracle of new life; the forest was not just a forest, but an ecosystem made up of individual trees and fascinating animals. Dogs were no longer dogs, but creatures who taught me about the exuberance of living and the humor of God. I learned that I had to wait until the chickens decided to lay their eggs before I could gather them. To go to town, I sometimes had to wait until a fallen tree had been rolled aside or the muddy road had dried up. This natural experience of waiting led to an intense awareness of the sacred. As the natural ground exploded into its harvest, so too my ground ignited with the divine fire. God was not only real but present.

In Nova Scotia I also learned of an ancient Jewish custom which changed my understanding of leisure. This custom regards the Sabbath as a time of presence. A vigil is held the preceding night to heighten our awareness and to usher in the Sabbath in a revered way. The Sabbath thus is neither a dutiful time of worship nor a day of rest. Instead, it becomes a day of true leisure, the celebration of reciprocity: we come to God and God comes to us. *Shekinah,* the divine indwelling, comes in a special way seeking human love. God chooses to linger with his creation and to have intercourse with it. "When that day comes, it is Yahweh who speaks, you will call me, 'my husband' " (Hos. 2:18). "I will betroth you to myself forever . . . with integrity and justice, with tenderness and love. I will betroth you to myself with faithfulness, and you will come to know Yahweh" (Hos. 2:21–22).

There is a celibate part of us that is in some way engaged to eternity, to holiness, to the God of all creativity. This part of us anticipates the footsteps of God's coming, sees the wonderful in the ordinary signs of his advent, and savors every glimpse of his being. When we come to recognize this celibate part of ourselves, I think we will spontaneously make special room in our lives for prolonged vigils and sacred days. These times will be so sacred that they can be gloriously celebrated, revered and, consequently, wasted.

By entering into this leisurely dimension of celibacy, I believe we will be better able to respond passionately to the whole of life. We will learn to be present to both the comedy and the tragedy, with both laughter and tears. We will become more real, more intensely saddened and more hilariously joyous, because of our faith that all these experiences are reconciled in God's presence. I think the absence of this faith is one reason why Jesus gets so angry with the Pharisees. "We played the pipes for you, and you wouldn't dance; we sang dirges and you wouldn't be mourners" (Mt. 11:17). They do not believe enough in God to let life seep into their bones and profoundly move them.

Jesus himself knows happiness and tears, gentleness and anger, harshness and compassion. What sustains and supports him in both positive and negative situations is his faith in God's presence. He can believe with Job that even in the darkest of nights he will again know laughter and the cries of joy (Jb 8:21). I sense in Jesus a conscious feeling not only of the rhythm of these alternating opposites but of their intrinsic harmony, their essential place in the eternal order. To respond to this divine order is, I believe, the essence of religious obedience. It is an interior and exterior sense of harmony, of being in step with the music, of doing the right thing at the right time. It is at once a listening and a response. Whenever I experience this harmony, I am filled with peace and joy. I am one with God, and this makes my heart light. My spirit soars; it yearns to express its delight. "You have made known the way of life to me; you fill me with gladness through your presence" (Ps. 16:11).

In each of the many saints I have read about, I can find some kind of playful attitude toward life. Granted, some of them are usually very serious and somber, but some saints are so lighthearted that they readily become the clown, the fool, the child. Francis of Assisi, for example, is so full of song and dance that he has become known as the troubadour of Christ, the crazy buffoon. Philip Neri does so many delirious things (such as cutting off only one side of his beard and moustache) that his contemporaries try to commit him to an insane asylum. John of the Cross, in his more serious love songs, and Teresa of Avila, in her rustic carols, both exhibit a sense of lighthearted oneness with the entire universe.

Lightheartedness, with its spirit of play, is often expressed in dance. Dancing has always been an excellent symbol of leisure, for it embodies all of the characteristics which also lead to creativity. To dance means to immerse our whole selves in the present moment. We focus our attention on the other, whether that other be a partner or the music or a particular rhythm, and we become one with the movement. Dancing has been regarded by many people as a waste of time, for when we are dancing we cannot do anything else. But that is precisely the point. And that is why dancing has always been an expression of divine worship and why I wish we would dance more in our liturgical services.

Sacred dances have been part of many different religious traditions. For the Sufis and the Shakers, in particular, the dance is an expression of the desire to serve God with the whole body and to enter into the rhythms of divine love. Far from being foolish, the dance brings us in tune with reality. As St. Augustine admits, it changes the pattern of our lives and is a means of vital union. "The dance, by its very nature, is ecstatic," Van der Leeuw writes. "It makes us beside ourself, lifts us above life and the world, and lets our whole earthly existence perish in the maelstrom."[12]

For the ancient Hebrews, dance was an expression not only of joy, but of intense praise. Only by wasting time, in losing oneself in the Beloved, can one really come to praise. The essence of real worship is the useless, selfless affirmation of the Other. Thus, when the Hebrews worshiped Yahweh, they put their whole heart and soul into it. "David and all the House of Israel danced before Yahweh with all their might, singing to the accompaniment of lyres, harps, tambourines, castinets, and cymbals. . . . David danced whirling round before Yahweh with all his might" (2 S. 6:5, 17). So lost was David in the frenzy of worship that he was "leaping and dancing before Yahweh . . . displaying himself as any buffoon" (2 S. 6:20).

There are other accounts of dances throughout the Old Testament. Many times there are processions, musicians, cantors, and maidens with tambourines. The book of Exodus speaks of timbrels and dancing (15:20–21); Judith writes of garlands and palm branches in the hands of all (15: 12–14); the first book of Samuel tells of dances to the sound of music and joyous cries (18:6). The Scriptures repeatedly invite us to praise God in a way that is more than verbal: "Praise my God with the tambourine, sing to the Lord with the cymbal; let psalms and canticles mingle for him, extol his name, invoke it" (Jdt. 16:1–2). "Let Israel rejoice in its maker and Zion's children exalt in their king; let them dance in praise of his name, playing to him on strings and drums" (Ps. 149:2–3).

The New Testament accounts are no different. Everywhere Jesus goes, he makes people lighthearted. "The blind see again, the lame walk, lepers are cleansed, and the deaf hear, the dead are raised to life" (Lk. 7:22). Through the ages, Christians have repeatedly come back to this concept of dance. Sixth-century Christian art portrays the resurrection of Jesus as a dance in which he draws the redeemed upward toward heaven. Christ, the firstborn of the dead, is the leader in the eschatology of freedom, and the Church, as his bride, dances along. According to these paintings, to dance is to see God. Dante, probably more than any other Christian writer, sees the entire universe laugh with delight in God's presence. He writes of innumerable dances.[13] Heaven is filled with "the dancing and great festival of the singing and the flashing of light with light, joyous and benign."[14] Everything for Dante whirls around the Center in perfect harmony and ecstatic rapture.

Implicit in a philosophy of creative leisure is the ability to receive. St. Paul tells us that, for the person who plays, everything is regarded as a gift (see 1 Co. 4:7). Receptivity and gratitude both seem to be essential attitudes for anyone who wants to grow spiritually and become more human. God always gives life as a gift; he gives freely of his time and his presence (see Rm. 6:23). We never earn his presence; we cannot work our way into heaven. Contemplative prayer is not utilitarian. It is simply time spent in mutual gift-giving.

I do not think that a real gift can be given in a utilitarian framework. If something is given with a certain purpose or gain in mind, it becomes a bribe rather than a real present. A gift, if it is genuine, is given out of love and for no purpose but to express love. The *ritardando* of prayer is sacred because there is no compulsion or expectations placed on either communicant. The gift of presence leaves both persons free, giving unrestricted play to all the creative and benevolent impulses that lie in their hearts.

I have stressed leisure and contemplation so much because they are essential to the process of becoming whole. Now I must put them in some perspective. We are not called to be passive, nor are we called to be active. We are not solely called to play or solely called to work. We are called to be creative. This call, which embraces activity and passivity, play and work, persists through life. Abraham Heschel puts it thus:

> The act of bringing the world into existence is a continuous process. God called the world into being and that call goes on. . . . Every instant is an act of creation. A moment is not a terminal but a flash, a signal of beginning. Time is perpetual innovation, a synonym for continuous creation.[15]

To become fully human, fully creative, we must embrace everything with an impassioned presence.

❧ 7. CELIBATE PASSION

> I have come to bring fire to the earth
> and wish that it were blazing already (Lk. 12:49).

CHEMISTRY has shown us that Gerard Manley Hopkins was right to find the world charged with God's grandeur. Each of us, both spiritually and physically, is a charged particle, an ion. As I pointed out in the last chapter, the more we are in dialogue with the world as "Thou," the greater is our charged energy. If we are truly present to reality, we cannot help but be on fire with intense passion, a passion for God, a passion for life, and a passion for others. We are body-soul beings who must continually give assent "to the warmth and strength and temper and passion of love."[1]

Sadly enough, both celibacy and passion have been badly misunderstood for centuries. Their meanings have been obscured and tainted by moral nuances, and have been, for the most part, obliterated with antiseptic, inhuman definitions. Although traditional Christian moralists have upheld celibacy as a virtue, they have certainly not presented it as very appealing. I often find their definitions of celibacy negative and empty. This celibacy seems to be merely the unripe virginal state, the incomplete situation of being unmarried and unloved. It is a sober, somber, bloodless virtue which represses or denies my basic sexuality. At the same time, however, attracted as I am to the enriching vitality of passion, I often find myself inhibited by passion's traditional definition of being mortally sinful: concupisence, lust, libido. This passion is irrational and animal; it somehow pertains to my weaker, "lower" self.

Although I am still trying to understand the place of celibacy and passion in my own life, I know that I value them both highly and I do not think they can be strictly opposed to one another. My celibacy has got to be passionate, and my passion, my desire for union with another, must have its celibate dimensions. Passion, as I experience it, is not something I consider dark or evil. It is a push, a drive from within, an energy which moves me into relationship with others. It is an intense thirst for intimacy, a yearning for real living, which at the same time affirms and accepts me as separate and individual. It is a passion which I hope will integrate all my inner forces into a single, fierce, and all-consuming love for heaven and for earth.

Celibate passion, I believe, is in every way the passion of eros. But eros, too, has been grossly misunderstood by our culture. This is partly due to the influence of Freud, who, in his early writings, identified eros with lust or libido. Quite understandably, whenever we now hear the word *erotic* we think of *erotica,* or pornography. In his later work, which has not yet been popularized, Freud makes a great distinction between the passion of libido and the passion of eros. Lust or libido is the biological drive toward coitus, a mere physical act. Eros, however, is the passion for relationship; it is the desire for goodness as much as for union and communion. Libido seeks release from physiological tension; its end point is the gratification of orgasm and its post-climatic relaxation. Eros, however, cherishes tension and seeks to sustain a homeostatic balance between relating opposites. Rollo May, in *Love and Will,* defines eros further:

> Eros is a desiring, longing, a forever reaching out, seeking to expand.
> . . . Eros seeks union with the other person in delight and passion, and
> the procreating of new dimensions of experience which broaden and
> deepen the being of both persons.[2]

Libido seeks a union of bodies with a definite termination as its aim. Eros seeks an intimacy of persons which continually entices them toward realms of infinite possibilities.

I really do not think that libidinous passion, which reduces "human sexuality to a purely biological function and the human person to a physical pleasure machine,"[3] has a place in the life of anyone striving to become more human and more religious. But I do believe that erotic passion must be present in anyone (the religious as well as the single or married lay person) who wishes to develop a mature and healthy relationship with God and with others. To be fully human seems to demand that we not only live fully in the present but that we continue to stretch and reach for what lies beyond us. Eros enables us to do this. As Erich Neumann, in *Amor and Psyche,* writes, eros is "the heat, the fire of passion, the flame and ardour of emotion that provides the basis of illumination"[4] and allows us to transcend ourselves. Eros is the life force of contemplation, true communion, and heroic sacrifice. As William McNamara writes, eros is the substance of real love:

> . . . the most dangerous thing in the world. It jeopardizes your safety, threatens your security, and turns your life inside out. It kills your cozy, puny, self-constructed little ego, but makes it possible for you to rise up . . . free for universal, cosmic love, which is the most noble but also the most exhausting human virtue.[5]

Eros is a passion more violent and more encompassing than libido. It is thus capable, I believe, of transforming any masculine-feminine relationship from a physical, sensual level to genuine ecstatic intimacy.

Without a doubt, the man-woman relationship is the most crucial horizontal relationship possible. Crucial in the sense that true union between the masculine and feminine must result in a precarious balance between the two, rather than in their fusion. I think one of the most seductive illusions of our age is the equation of coitus with undivided oneness of being. The sirens of society continuously whisper that sexual union will satisfy our desires for wholeness. Generally, we do not learn of our deception until libido has utterly failed to meet its promises. Even in the physiological spasms of orgasm, we remain separate and distinct from one another.

In a relationship between a man and a woman, erotic passion moves toward their union, but at the same time maintains their individual uniqueness. Eros seeks no termination, no "melting pot," no absorption, but rather it relishes the continual attraction between male and female. This type of relationship is entirely foreign to that of libido, which tries to tempt us into forgetting the "ion-ness" of our beings. The contemporary rage for *co*-everything in human relationships—compromise, cooperation, coexistence, cohabitation—typifies libido's attempt to obliterate the nun, the existential solitary in each of us. Eros tells us that real intimacy is no compromise, but a communion between two solitaries who, as Rainer Maria Rilke writes, "protect and touch and greet each other."[6] Such intimacy demands a radical death of the ego, a "coming-un-I-on" process, with a simultaneous increase in awareness of the other as distinct and loving. Erotic union stimulates us to greater participation; libidinous union lulls us to sleep.

The capacity for intimacy with another person seems to depend on the capacity for intimacy with ourselves and with God. Without passion, our interpersonal relationships are shallow. The eros of God arouses in us a passion which is greater than any flame we could produce by ourselves. "My heart grew hot within me," says the psalmist, "and as I meditated, a certain fire was enkindled" (Ps. 38:4). What is distinct about divine-human eros is that it becomes increasingly powerful. The closer we get to God, like the chemist's ionic bond, the greater is the passion which flows through us. Intimacy with God in this life is neither an exclusive nor a terminal relationship. It charges us with ever more energy so that we may be vital conductors of God's irresistible love.

To be intimate with ourselves (quite unlike the type of masturbation which merely seeks physical release from tension) means to know ourselves so well that we can let go of ourselves. Like intimacy with God, this intimacy is a definite "un-I-on" process. We learn to let go of everything which sustains the ego and maintains rancid narcissism. Real prayer and real love effect a monumental transformation in which the I-on (eye on myself) becomes the eye-on (eye on the other). In this form of intimacy, the other increases while we decrease (refer to Jn. 3:30). But in decreasing, we are not obliterated. By annihilating our egos, by seeking death instead of survival, we paradoxically receive the gift of God's presence: true life (Rm. 6:23). The more empty we become, the more dynamically we rush headlong into the infinite completeness of a fuller and more abundant life (Jn. 10:10).

I firmly believe that the person who meditates and who finds God in the solitude of prayer will not only reach a new level of awareness of others, but will achieve a new freedom of relationship to these others. St. Teresa is quick to tell us that persons who are immersed in God will not be sterile or dispassionate in their dealings with others. "No," she says, "they will love others much more than they did, with a more genuine love, with greater passion and with a love which brings more profit; that, in a word, is what love really is."[7] William Johnston, in his book *Silent Music*, adds:

> Meditation, far from weakening, may liberate one's sexual energy. . . . But together with this liberation comes a power and a self-mastery (and this is chastity) which enables people to express their love sexually when it is appropriate to do so and to refrain from physical expression when circumstances so demand. And to do so in such a way that their love, rooted at the deep core of their being, never grows old.[8]

The man-woman relationship that is erotic but not coital could be the greatest single witness to society of the inadequacies of mere libido. This, I think, is one of the reasons why men and women who accept their innate celibacy are so desperately needed in today's world. These men and women stand apart from the common stream of humanity and face the reality of solitariness head-on. They can stand alone, in need, accepting that need, and refusing to manipulate God or another person to satisfy it. Their lives and their loves tell us that true freedom implies separation and uniqueness. True intimacy involves, first, a wholeness from within, and second, a sensitivity to the other person, with no infringement upon his or her individuality. The persons who have integrated within themselves the opposing masculine and femine forces will discover the truth of Erich Fromm's contention that "the ability to be alone is the condition for the ability to love."[9]

A mistake many in today's society make is to substitute the coital man-woman relationship for the person-God relationship. In striving for full human maturity and individuality, some of us have mistaken the lure of libido as the passion of eros. We have erroneously believed that sexual intercourse must be the only and the inevitable conclusion of our various expressions of sexuality. Instead of relating creatively to the other, we have merely entered the impersonal mainstream of Mother Nature's drive for biological preservation of the species.

Indeed, intimacy with God can keep expressions of our intimacy with each other within appropriate limits. However, erotic intimacy is never an easy thing to achieve nor is it ever safe. As St. Teresa says, we must place ourselves unconditionally in the hands of the beloved. We must be completely open to a presence that demands death, that demands total surrender to the transforming fires of love. We must enter into a closeness that demands detachment, so that the beloved may be forever enlivened and freed to "grow maturely into the full stature of Christ" (Eph. 4:13).

Being intimate is the vocation of every person, single or married, lay or cleric. It is the most human behavior possible, and simultaneously, the most divine. At the same time, however, we fear intimacy more than anything else, and rightly so. As Irene de Castillejo points out, with intimacy there is always "the fear of being taken advantage of, and the terror of possible involvement which we had never intended."[10] Intimacy with God or with another person can become too much to bear. It is like a cosmic electricity, a totally free and universal energy that threatens to destroy us.

Christ is a lightning bolt that knocks people off their horses. He burns away our facades; he ravages and shocks, thunders and roars. He reminds us that we cannot be comfortable with God, for if we feel at ease, then it is not God to whom we are relating, but ourselves. If we are spiritually at ease, then we are like static mannikins. We have become lifeless. If we truly pray we can never get used to Christ or ever be comfortable with God. Their eros, their spirit, is a fire of unstoppable burning.

Because we are intent upon survival, on maintaining our egos, we necessarily rubberize our existence. We pad ourselves, hoping to shield ourselves from intimacy and from giving ourselves totally to another. Like the society in which we live, we seem to condomize everything. We use prophylactics even with God. We may give parts of ourselves, but seldom or never wholeheartedly and unreservedly. We are not reckless enough to bare our souls. We are not mad enough to strip completely and go all the way to Golgotha. Once we let God or another person move, touch, and electrify us, the damage is done. There is no going back.

I think one of the reasons we are so afraid to expose ourselves to another is connected to our utilitarian way of conceiving things. We have grown so accustomed to an aggressive, exploitative way of life that we suspect, and expect, the same aggression and exploitation in every man-woman encounter. Progress has become our new god. Each particular expression of a relationship is thought to be a step in an inevitable progression. This presumption has been central to the thinking of traditional moral theology; there is supposed to be an "inevitable progression from flitting image to welcome fantasy, to elaborated daydream, to sexual arousal, to masturbation or sexual intercourse."[11] Everything in our present mentality is geared toward progression toward orgasm. It is both sad and terribly uncreative, I think, that so many of us believe that love must be expressed by the full completion of this succession.

Like many of my contemporaries, I learned the biological and chemical facts of sexual physiology from the work of Masters and Johnson. Their contribution to the scientific field has been invaluable, but their statistics and tape measures can be an enormous hindrance to real eros and genuine intimacy. There is a danger in our society of making technique an end in itself, and of consciously or unconsciously comparing oneself to a statistical average. We often seem to be more worried about performance and timing than we are with developing a deep and unique relationship. William McNamara agrees:

> We no longer engage in the exquisitely delicate, prolonged, and ecstatic artistry of "making love"; we just matter of factly "have sex"; we don't thoughtfully enter into "intercourse," that profound and purifying process, we "screw" or "ball" a "chick"; we don't "go to bed," a marvelous phrase connoting holy leisure and wise passiveness, we "lay" someone or get "laid."[12]

We desiccate passion whenever we use sex as a means to our own sexual gratification and pleasure. Where sex becomes utilitarian, eros is destroyed. As Rollo May remarks, "By anesthetizing feeling in order to perform better, by employing sex as a tool to prove prowess and identity, by using sensuality to hide sensitivity, we have emasculated sex and left it vapid and empty."[13] Furthermore, we desecrate ourselves and one another by the overuse of technology and technique. All too easily can we become psychologically and spiritually castrated, with feelings of despair and of having been used.

If I were to advocate a heightened awareness of celibate passion while maintaining a utilitarian philosophy, I would have to insist that we meet strict and rigid standards in our interpersonal relationships. No embrace, no kiss, no touch would ever be allowed, because to permit any of them would be considered a consent to the whole act to which these were preludes.[14] Such rigidity is quite different from the love Jesus lives out. His love is fully sensuous and spontaneously tactile. But it centers on whole-personed intimacy and relishes each expression of communication as an end in itself. The effects of such love are stunning. His erotic love for Magdalen irreversibly shocks her from libido. His passion arouses others from their apathy.

Erotic celibate passion involves a leisurely attitude toward another which does not seek to dominate or exploit. It necessitates a contemplative reverence for the beloved and an acceptance of each expression of intimacy for itself, with no thought of inevitable progression. So few of us today have this sense of leisure that this form of love-making may well be confined to a very small number of persons, persons, I am quite sure, who know the meaning of such love from their experience of prayer. In *Nature, Man and Woman,* Alan Watts writes of such love-making:

> Contemplative love, like contemplative meditation, . . . has no specific aim; there is nothing particular that has to be made to happen (e.g. it does not purposely aim at orgasm). . . . In a relationship which has no goal other than itself, nothing is merely preliminary. One finds out what it can mean simply to look at the other person, to touch hands, or listen to the voice. . . . The psychic counterpart of this bodily and sensuous intimacy is a similar openness of attention to each other's thoughts, a form of communion which can be as sexually "charged" as physical contact. This is the feeling that one can express one's thoughts to the other just as they are, since there is not the slightest compulsion to assume a pretended character. This is perhaps the rarest and most difficult aspect of any human relationship. . . . Yet this is quite the most important part of a deep sexual relationship and it is in some way understood even when thoughts are left unsaid. . . . To unveil the flow of thought can therefore be an even greater sexual intimacy than physical nakedness.[15]

Although the troubadours of the Middle Ages were not necessarily contemplatives, they were acquainted with the philosophy of leisure. Thus a practice of courtly erotic love developed quite separately from the tradition of procreative, orgasmic love associated with marriage. No behavior of this courtly love was regarded as "foreplay"; everything was considered in the light of a leisurely, playful expression of intimacy.

> Even in the final stage, the behavior of the lover and his lady was, by most standards, curious, if not altogether improbable. For they were very likely to indulge repeatedly in protracted sessions of sex play, unclothed and in bed, without yielding to the imperious drive toward completion. . . . And scores of rhapsodists of *l'amour courtois* scorned the culmination of the sex act as false love while extolling as true love the pure kissing, touching, fondling, and naked contact of the lovers.[16]

Prolonged coital union was indeed present in these relationships, but if historians are correct on this matter, it was *coitus reservatus,* coitus without orgasm.

The purpose of medieval erotic love was not a mere physical feat, but the opening of two persons to an intimate oneness. Orgasm is not the only way, and is not even necessarily *a* way, of achieving this whole-personed communion. Herbert Richardson, in *Nun, Witch, Playmate,* points out that conversation, the honest sharing of one's heart, mind, and spirit, was considered by the courtly lovers as a greater expression of intimacy than coitus. Thus, kissing on the mouth was considered the highest form of physical affection.

> Genital union is a way of uniting only bodies but kissing is a way of uniting oneself with that part of the body that is the organ of the soul. Through the mouth, not through the genitals, the true intercourse between a man and woman is created. Hence the act of kissing is the act of honoring and loving the organ through which spiritual communion is sustained.[17]

In his *Treatise on Spiritual Friendship,* the twelfth-century abbot Aelred of Rievaulx writes about three types of kisses: the bodily physical kiss, the kiss of the spirit or of Christ (the union of hearts), and the kiss of the mind (infusion of grace into the soul through God). Courtly love may not have always resulted in heightened spirituality, but it did aim at intimacy and reverence between whole persons.

I am not suggesting that all expressions of courtly erotic behavior are always appropriate and moral in a relationship between any man and any woman. However, I am suggesting that all of our love-making, regardless of who we are or what we are committed to, should be purposeless and leisurely. In an erotic relationship involving singles, vowed religious, or two people not married to each other, abstinence from intercourse can be one expression of such leisurely love. Likewise, in the erotic relationship of married persons who do not desire children, abstinence from orgasm can be a viable alternative to artifical means of contraception. The desire for communion in selfless erotic love cannot be the desire to possess or "own" another. Action which progresses to orgasm, especially in the relationships just mentioned, may abort the limitless creativity which lies in the man-woman relationship.

Celibate passion does require discipline. Without such control, eros would easily dissipate into lust. Anne Morrow Lindbergh comments:

> Intimacy is tempered by lightness of touch. We have moved through our day like dancers, not needing to touch more than lightly because we instinctively move to the same rhythm. . . . To touch heavily would be to arrest the pattern and freeze the movement, to check the endlessly changing beauty of its unfolding. There is no place for the possessive clutch, the clinging arm, the heavy hand; only the barest touch in passing.[18]

Erotic intimacy requires freedom, uniqueness, and a certain amount of separation. To love leisurely is to acknowledge with Lao Tzu that too much tasting can become distasteful and overexposure may kill pleasure.

> Doing spoils it, grabbing misses it;
> So the Wise Man refrains from doing
> And doesn't spoil anything;
> He grabs at nothing and so never misses.[19]

Moral uprightness is indeed needed for such intimate love-making. We must carefully discern whether our expressions of love for another are conducive to the creative growth and actualization of both. Besides the discipline of meditation and the purification of asceticism, values such as honesty, self-liberation, enrichment of others, fidelity, and social responsibility are extremely important to consider in our choice of sexual expression.[20] Poverty and simplicity are also, I am finding, intrinsic characteristics of celibate passion. For such love is not the meeting of our accumulated possessions, but the sharing of who we are. Intimacy is a special gift between persons who, having stripped themselves of all externals, give lavishly of their essential and deepest selves.

Intimacy is not the summation of our attachments, but the

expression and result of our detachments. Until we rid ourselves of all our superficial holdings and feverish activities, we are too complicated to be intimate and too encumbered to be lovers. We cannot fully embrace God or another person unless we first let go of our attachments. Intimacy is the simplicity of a pilgrim; eros is the flight of a sparrow that is no longer tied down. The freedom and lightness of having nothing allows us to be more joyously in love with all things and all persons. Perhaps this is why Jesus says to his apostles, "Take with yourselves no gold or silver, no haversack or spare tunic, no footwear or staff" (Mt. 10:9–10). If we are burdened by anything, we cannot spend ourselves freely. If we are concerned about our possessions, we will not be able to focus solely and simply on the other.

True love makes us poor. An encounter with the beloved always astounds us and fills us with an overwhelming sense of unworthiness. Moments of leisurely intimacy remind us that we do not deserve them. Our inner poverty screams from every fiber of our being, and we wonder how another can love us so completely. Although we realize that who we are and what we bring to the other will never be enough, such love requires the gift of our innermost self, and demands that we sacrifice everything for the beloved. St. John of the Cross writes in *Living Flame of Love*: "The true lover is content only when all that he is and all that he is worth and can be worth, and all that he has and can have, are employed in the Beloved; and the more of this there is, the greater is the pleasure that he receives in giving it."21

The celibate lover not only sacrifices everything for the other, but becomes the embodiment of this sacrifice. By refraining from the temptation to receive something in return, to possess the other, to become satisfied, the celibate may have to sacrifice his or her own body. To refuse to use the beloved in any way may mean to refuse to satisfy one's own physiological needs. To be celibate love-makers, I am beginning to realize, we must always leave the other untouched and virginal. This virginity may or may not be physical; it may perhaps be psychological or spiritual. But there are sacred areas in the other which, because they are reserved for

God alone, we can never enter. We must, in this sense, come to the other with empty hands and come away with empty hands. Nonpossession is essential to celibate passion.

Our love for one another must never interfere with or detract from our love relationship with God. Furthermore, we must respect the other's integrity by doing everything possible to keep God's love growing and burning within him or her. Jesus himself shows us that deep human relationships must always be intertwined with a love-life with God. Detachment, for him, is never an ascetic practice for the sake of self-depravation; it is the generous gift to God of what is most intimate and precious to him.

Although asceticism is a necessary discipline for all expressions of celibate passion, Jesus instructs us not to become enamored of our ascetical accomplishments. Jesus denounces the Pharisees because they stop at the level of detachment and never attain the real compassion and generosity of eros. "When you fast," Jesus says, "do it quietly. . . . When you give alms, do not let your right hand know what your left is doing. . . . When you pray, do it in secret" (Mt. 6:16,3,6). Eros does not lie in the discipline itself, but in its ability to spur us on to a more open and selfless gift of ourselves. Ultimately, we must be detached from the detachment itself. Note, however, that this further discipline does not mean that we stop being ascetics, or ease up on the discipline. Jesus does not say "if you fast, give alms and pray," but rather "when you fast, give alms, and pray." Attitudinal detachment is only born and sustained by a persistent existential expression of poverty. To become simple, in our hearts and in our relationships, I think we must strip ourselves in some way each day.

Jesus' life gives evidence of the importance of actual poverty, but always as a means to greater passion. His entire public ministry is a progression in simplicity and intimacy. His focus during the forty days he spends in the "Lenten" desert is on coming to terms with the meaning of poverty. His deliberate refusal to embrace any security—economic, personal, sexual, or political—strengthens him to flesh out the values of poverty (and also of eros) gradually and persistently. In St. Matthew's Gospel we read

that Jesus stresses the necessity of emotional and sensuous detachment. We must (and the Hindus agree) relinquish even our crav-
ings, desires, and appetites (see Mt. 5:29–48). Furthermore, we
must rid ourselves of all material possessions. Jesus has no money,
no home, no family. He has no extra clothes, no luxuries of any
kind (Mt. 6:24; 8:20–21; 10:13).

I think another type of poverty which is crucial to celibate
passion concerns temporal and volitional detachment. Jesus'
agony in the garden is a decisive movement from attachment to
his own plans to total simplicity. The crucifixion, with its pain and
mockery, its nakedness and humiliation, not only strips Jesus of
all possible human possessions but prepares him for the last and
hardest detachment. Moments before his death, he must free himself from all spiritual attachments, even from the presence of God.

Because Jesus has so perfectly freed himself from everything, he
can give himself perfectly, wholly and completely as no other
love-sacrifice has ever been given. His love act is so fierce and total
that for all time an entire universe of others can be made one.
Intimacy with God and with other persons now becomes a possibility and reality. This intimacy is the goal and meaning of Christi-
anity; detachment and poverty are ways to this end.

One of the subtle dangers of our age involves the sophisticated
way we approach the Gospel message of detachment. We no
longer interpret literally Jesus' words to leave behind everything.
We reason that detachment is primarily an attitude, and therefore,
we do not consider our material wealth, numerous possessions,
and middle-class indulgences as harmful. It is true that our material possessions are good in themselves and that having them does
not necessarily mean we are attached to them. Nevertheless, I find
a danger, insidious but real, in surrounding ourselves with many
things. Abundance tends to weary and dull us.

Examples of this abound. Too much seeing may lead to eye
strain or blurred vision. Too much talking may produce strained
vocal cords. Too much listening may prevent hearing or may stimulate daydreaming. Too much food usually makes us drowsy.
Alcohol in excess dulls our reflexes. Sexual orgasm results in sleep.

We are not necessarily overindulgent (for oversatiation usually has a noticeable unhealthy effect and we do something to correct it). What concerns me is that constant fullness may produce in us unnoticed, and hence uncorrected, effects such as dullness, mediocrity, and indifference.

For a vibrantly loving eroticism, both Jesus and John of the Cross stress the importance of being empty. If we are attached to anything other than God, we are not true disciples (Mt. 10:37–39). "The soul that has attachment to anything, however much virtue it possess, will not attain to the liberty of Divine Union."[22] "How complete must be the detachment of our soul from all things if it is to journey to God."[23] I think these messages are meant to be taken quite literally. We may agree that we can eliminate and discipline ourselves about things we merely *want.* However, we are not so ready to relinquish things we *need.* We say that needs are part of being human and that they must be met in order for us to be healthy. This seems to me to be a middle-class way of living poverty.

A really poor person lives in need. Religiously poor persons acknowledge their perpetual neediness before God and so choose to live as witnesses of that fact. Nothing on this earth (not even our present experience of God) will be able to satisfy and fill us as completely as our final eternal union with the Divine. Over and over again, by his example and by his teaching, Jesus bears witness to this celibacy by his poverty. He tells us that human solutions to our needs do not satisfy us. God alone can satisfy, and he will always fill the person who is in need. If we are hungry, he becomes our bread; if we are thirsty, he is our wine; when we are alone, he is our companion; when we are rejected, he will love us with an everlasting love.

Christian detachment, because of the incarnational dimension of God, is not a rejection or disdain for the world or for the flesh but a stripping away of encumbrances so that eros may grow stronger in us. By detaching ourselves from many things we may become more clearly singlehearted and apprehend intimacy more completely. We become detached only to become more attached.

The stronger our detachment and our desire for intimacy, the more courageous and faithful we will be to the erotic stretching required to reach God through, with, and in each other.

The purity of mind and heart which results from this erotic stretching allows us to be as sensual as we are spiritual. And paradoxically, sensuality and spirituality become the same thing. Celibate passion may be nonpossessive, but it is intimately involved. This delicate balance entails a priority in our personal commitments and a sensitivity to possible scandal, while at the same time it expresses a profound love for the other. This balance does not mean that there will be no desire for coital union. Rather, as Viktor Frankl argues, this erotic passion "is independent of the body to the extent that it does not need the body. . . . Where sexuality is possible, love will desire and seek it; but where renunciation is called for, love will not necessarily cool or die."[24] True love will grow through and beyond the physical to encompass both persons in God. Thus I believe that both unmarried and married lovers can come to genuine sexual freedom and real intimacy with each other. Teilhard de Chardin shares this same dream:

> Love is in the process of undergoing a metamorphosis. . . . Some day, after mastering the winds, the waves, the tides, and gravity, we shall harness for God the energies of love. And then, for the second time in the history of the world, we will have discovered fire.[25]

Eros does not neglect the physical, but exceeds it by encompassing and transcending it.

☯ 8. EROTIC INTIMACY

THE masculine-feminine polarity has been so consciously felt in human history that it seems to underlie the thought of all ages. Ish, the masculine principle of fire, is indeed wedded to Esh, the feminine principle of earth. One of Carl Jung's great contributions to psychiatry is the demonstration that individual wholeness involves the integration of the masculine and feminine principles inside us. Only by becoming integrated may we stand apart from the crowd as individuals, as solitaries, as celibates. Only through the purifying process of this individuation will we be able to achieve integrity. What Jung speaks of is the essence of celibate passion. It is the *hieros gamos,* the inner marriage of the Sol (man) and Luna (woman) inside each of us. It is the reconciliation of our inner animus and anima.

Jesus' command to love others as we love ourselves reminds us that we must indeed know ourselves before we can give ourselves away in selfless love. Traditionally, virginity and celibacy have always been thought to lead the person to an increased awareness of self. Virginity and celibacy, however, contain the temptation to be content with ourselves, to fall into narcissism. Jesus, as virgin and celibate, transcends this temptation in the sacrifice of himself on the cross. In this sacrifice, the earth of his body is wedded to the fire of death, and eternal salvation is won. I think what makes Jesus' sacrifice so perfect is not only his sinlessness and the purity of his passion for divine union but also the universality of his death act. He integrates in his being all possibilities: the human and the divine, the masculine and the feminine, the just and the merciful, the intellectual and the emotional. These he offers in himself wholly (holy) to God.

The eucharistic liturgy (the sacrifice of Christ), as Jung presents it, is a symbol of the celibate wholeness required of each of us. At one time in church history, when mandatory confession preceded Mass, the imagery of wholeness was much clearer. The self-examination of the confession was considered an integral part of the Mass ritual. It was a time to know and integrate oneself, so that one could really enter into communion with God. Today, the symbolism, though less vivid, remains the same. We are called to integrate the masculine and feminine within us by acknowledging and affirming as gifts from God these aspects of our personality. The bread, the body, signifies the eternal feminine: the dying and rising, the darkness and desolation of life. The wine, the blood, is all that is masculine: the ecstasy and the illumination, the consuming union. In the consecration of bread and wine, we understand that we are not just masculine or feminine; we are both.

Throughout history, androgynous or hermaphroditic imagery has always been associated with the celibate. The reason for this, I think, is that if I am only feminine, then I am only half; if I am only masculine, I am incomplete. In either case I limit the ways I can be intimate with God and with others. Hermaphroditic imagery suggests an inner state of consciousness in which the animus and the anima have become one. There is within me a reconciliation of opposites, a sacred *coniunctio,* in which all relationships and all experiences become erotic. *The Gospel According to Thomas,* a gnostic text of the second century, affirms the necessity of this inner marriage for any type of intimacy.

They said to Him: "Shall we then, being children, enter the kingdom?" Jesus said to them: "When you make the two one, and when you make the inner as the outer and the outer as the inner and the above as the below, and when you make the male and the female into a single one, so that the male will not be male and the female not be female . . . then shall you enter the kingdom."[1]

Without this meeting of opposites, we cannot be whole, nor can there be any chance for real love to break through.

Because each of us, to some degree, is celibate, each of us is also, it seems, androgynous. The existence of this core or center of the masculine-feminine polarity is what allows us to be intimate with all persons, regardless of their sex. We are all bisexual, homosexual, and heterosexual, and to limit these words or experiences to a mere physical level of expression is, in my opinion, to demean intimacy and our very humanness. Erotic bisexuality involves a passion for intimacy which does not have to be expressed in a genital way. Interpersonal oneness is achieved because each person shares his or her own inner oneness.

In our twentieth-century society which is just awakening to the women's movement, bisexuality (the masculine–feminine polarity of all relationships) is becoming an important concern. Certainly, union between two persons regardless of their sex has always had religious connotations.[2] But what I have been discovering is that the interpersonal union which we fantasize, advertise, and capitalize upon is but an expression of a deeper intrapersonal union for which we yearn. So deep is this second union that ancient mythologies and theologies have visualized it as God. In some traditions, God is hermaphroditic; in others, as in the Roman and Greek mythologies, he is split into gods and goddesses.

In Hindu literature, the masculine-feminine polarity is presented as two aspects of God: Brahma, the creator of light, and Shiva, the dark destroyer. On one level, each of these divine personalities is considered masculine with a female counterpart. Brahma is united with Viraj; together they produce the concrete universe. The consort of Shiva, who also acts as his spokeswoman, is, according to Puranic literature, Maha-maya, Sati, or Parvati. Through her sexual union with Shiva, Parvati becomes the mother of the world inevitably doomed to end. She, too, is a destroyer, an angel of death, a mistress of illusion. On another level of Hindu tradition, Brahma is masculine while Shiva is regarded as feminine. They are united in a third personality of the Godhead, that of the androgynous preserver, Vishnu.

The earliest Chinese literature, which dates from a matriarchal society, presents the deity in the form of the Mother Goddess Nai-Nai. She is the patroness of all living things, especially in pregnancy, childbirth, and fate. Later in Chinese history, when the culture becomes patriarchal, the deity becomes Tao, the Way, with its famous Yin-Yang polarity. In his poetry, Lao Tzu tells us that the Mother Goddess is still alive in this new masculine culture. "The valley spirit is not dead; they say it is the mystic female. Her gateway is, they further say, the base of earth and heaven."[3] Furthermore, Lao Tzu says, this same feminine principle is to be found in every man. "Everyone knows this, that weakness prevails over strength and that gentleness conquers."[4] "The female principle, as softness and pliableness, is associated with life and survival. Because he can yield, a man can survive."[5] To become whole, each male must encounter his female principle.

In Judaism, we find both masculine and feminine counterparts in Yahweh. This is alluded to in Genesis several times. "God said: 'Let us make man in our own image, in the likeness of ourselves. . . . God created man in the image of himself, in the image of God he created him, male and female he created them" (Gn. 1:26–27). Although God (Elohim) is masculine, his Spirit (ruah) is feminine. This Spirit is his creative command, his life-giving principle. It is a gentle wind (see 2 S. 22:11; Ps. 18:11; Ho. 4:19; Ps. 104:4), and the evidence of God's presence (see Ps. 139:7; Ws. 1:7; Is. 63:10).

In the New Testament, Jesus is indeed masculine, complete with righteous anger, political involvements, and an all-male ingroup of disciples. But at the same time, he is presented as feminine: loving the sinner, nursing the sick, enjoying the child, and feeding the hungry. Christ is both animus and anima: the masculine Logos of intelligence and cognition and the feminine Eros of loving relationships. Christ, as Carl Jung perceives, is androgynous. He is the masculine Word of God, and at the same time, he is the feminine spirit of wisdom (refer to 1 Co. 1:18, 22, 24; 2:2, 7–10).

Various Christian writers have continued to present the feminine aspect of God. St. Anselm is one. The most interesting writer on this issue I have encountered, is the fourteenth-century mystic, Juliana of Norwich. In defining her experience of God, she presents the first person as the masculine truth or Father. The second person, Christ, is feminine, the Mother of wisdom, mercy, understanding, and restoration. "Our Savior is our true Mother, in whom we are endlessly born; and we shall never come out of him. . . . Jesus Christ is our Mother. We have our being in him, there, where the ground of Motherhood begins."[6] For Juliana, the third person of the Trinity is neither masculine nor feminine, but neutral: the Lord of love and grace.

> God almighty is our kindly Father: and God all-wisdom is our kindly Mother: with the love and goodness of the Holy Ghost; which is all one God, one Lord. . . . He is the Ground: he is the substance: he is the very thing called kindness. And he is the very Father and the very Mother of natures.[7]

What excites me about Juliana is her identification of the second person, Christ, as feminine. This has vast implications, not only in coming to terms with the feminine side of our beings, but in realizing that a woman, as much as a man, can be Christ. To me, Juliana's vision not only supports women's role in the Church, but elevates women to the same priestly ministry which we Westerners have limited to males. The woman (as well as the man) who has achieved an inner union of wholeness, has a very special role to play in the psychological and spiritual development of our society. She is the *soror mystica* of Dante, whose passion elevates us to Paradise. She is the one who leads us to God, the one who strengthens us for heaven.[8] Her erotic love awakens within us the passion of agápe. C. S. Lewis describes such a woman: "Few men looked on her without becoming, in a certain fashion, her lovers. But it was the kind of love that made them not less, but truer, to their own wives."[9] Such a woman leads us into full intimacy with the entire universe.

Transformation into a complete individual is an arduous task which must be accomplished alone, but never in a vacuum. The ancient alchemists believed that the great work of individuation could not be done by earth alone, but only by earth in combination with fire. No one can possibly hope to obtain this union "unless there be some person sent by God to instruct him in it."[10] St. Ambrose, in *De Institutione Virginis,* declares that man without woman (and this may also be understood at the psychological level within an individual) is physically and spiritually incomplete. Woman is the "glory" of man, his spiritual completion, his grace. Without her, man cannot fully obtain his true being in Christ.[11] Man needs woman to be his spiritual guide as much as woman needs man for the same journey toward integration.

One of my biggest hopes for the Church is that in the next ten years new opportunities will open up for religious men and women to work side by side as healers and humanizers. Not only do I hope men and women can come closer in a working situation, I hope they will even be able to live together in the same community. I say this based on my own experience and on my belief in intimate adult relationships that are grounded in prayer, supported by a shared vision, and built on mutual respect. I think the present living options in religious life are not broad enough. Sometimes they dichotomize the masculine and the feminine into opposing camps, instead of reconciling them into a viable union. Instead of all-women convents and all-men rectories or monasteries, I hope that mixed communities (men and women, cleric and lay) will soon become feasible.

I have had the privilege of living both in a convent and in a mixed community. Although both options have their problems and joys, I know that the masculine-feminine situation generates for me more life, more love, and more prayer. Critics of mixed communities (many of whom have never lived in one) will argue that the tendency of eros to demand full genital expression is almost inevitable when men and women live together in community. My experience does not confirm this. True, in a mixed community masculine-feminine pairing does tend to occur. But this tendency is neither good nor bad in itself. In some cases of pairing, the relationship can become so introverted and exclusive that it is not good for the entire group; but in many of the cases I have witnessed, the personal love of such relationships thrusts the two people even more effectively into the community and into the apostolate. I might add that pairing, both heterosexual and homosexual, is also a phenomenon that can and does occur in any convent or in any monastery.

Granted, the man or woman who is passionate walks a fine line between eros and libido. Walking this line always presents the possibility of failure. C. S. Lewis, in speaking of the man-woman relationship, is keenly aware of this possibility:

> There's something in natural affection which will lead it on to eternal love more easily than natural appetite could be led on. But there's also something in it which makes it easier to stop at the natural level and mistake it for the heavenly. Brass is mistaken for gold more easily than clay is. And if it finally refuses conversion, its corruption will be worse than the corruption of what ye call the lower passions. It is a stronger angel, and therefore, when it falls, a fiercer devil.[12]

Although we must be aware of this danger, we must not let the fear of failure make us impotent or frigid. If we spend enough time in contemplation of the other in his or her entirety, we will not only see the person, but also the many relationships and commitments that already bind him or her, ties that may be necessary for that person's full freedom and growth. If we really love the other, we will desire to enter into his or her truth. To share only part of ourselves or to express our love in a way which ignores all of these other relationships in the beloved's life, is not honest. It is, it seems to me, libidinous deceit, pure selfishness, basic sin.

I do not think that persons who have realized the celibate part of themselves and who then happen to fall in love with each other, can with full integrity just fall into bed. How far they go in physical expression and what they do together must be a deliberate, mutual decision which encompasses the reality of their conscience, reason, and primary commitments. Their intimacy must be erotic instead of libidinous; their love most overflow from an abundance that desires communion, rather than an emptiness which needs to be filled up. Although such love may be difficult to maintain, I believe that the intensity of prayer and the strength of one's sense of commitment to spouse, community, other friends, or to one's ideal self are two essential factors which can keep any sexual expression from becoming inordinate.

Loving too much can never be a problem. However, we can misinterpret the meaning of passion and let it lure us into modes of expression which reveal that we really do not love enough. A celibate lover loves an an integrated whole. Body and soul are so wedded that expressions of one are the expressions of the other. Thus there can be real freedom; there can be St. Augustine's "love and do what you will." A celibate lover cannot be detached or dispassionate. (Dispassion is one of the grievous sins of our age. Too many of us have detached our minds from our bodies). He or she has to be so integrated that everything does matter.

Erotic celibate intimacy may or may not preserve physical virginity, but it does maintain the original meaning of *virginity*. As Alan Watts explains, a *parthenos,* or virgin, was a man or women who was fully responsible, integrated, and whole, a person in his or her own right.[13] Chastity is indeed a requirement of erotic celibate love, but I agree wholeheartedly with the 1977 report on human sexuality commissioned by the Catholic Theological Society of America that chastity is

> ... that virtue which enables a person to transform the power of human sexuality into a creative and integrative force in his or her life. It facilitates the fullest realization of one's being as male or female and encourages the integration of self with others in the human community. Chastity makes possible both intrapersonal and interpersonal development calling for an active response to the possibilities that human sexuality offers.[14]

The key to both physical virginity and sexual intercourse is their fertility. In erotic intimacy, procreation must happen. This procreation, however, is never limited to bodily pregnancy. Celibate passion conceives and brings to birth the limitless forms of new life residing within the other. This love nurtures fruitful relationships, dormant talents, and the infant soul of the beloved. One of the greatest examples of this type of lover is the French saint, Joan of Arc. Here is a virgin, the only woman in a camp of soldiers, who lives, eats, and sleeps with men, and then leads them into battle. She is extremely prayerful and utterly passionate, and yet she chooses to remain virginal. She and her male companions both know that if their relationship becomes too exclusive, if sexual intercourse is allowed to occur, some greater procreation will be aborted.

What I am saying should not be equated with the usual concept of Platonic love. Celibate passion, erotic intimacy, is not sexless or bodiless. It is a love so real and so enormous that it takes us to, through, and beyond the physical to more embracing forms of relationship and freedom. Instead of the enslavement of libido, erotic intimacy drives us to the brink of divine love. We are freed to touch God and to touch the other person. Here is how Dante expresses it:

> No heart was ever so disposed to devotion
> and with more complete assent
> so readily to give itself up to God
> as I became at these words,
> and all my love was so set on Him
> that it eclipsed Beatrice in oblivion.
> This did not displease her; she smiled.[15]

Beatrice loved Dante by refusing to satisfy his immediate needs, and thus, by calling him to transcend his human limitations. Dante understands the meaning of this love, and after his lady has led him into Paradise, he expresses to her his thanks:

> You have lifted me from slavery to freedom
> by all those ways, by all the means
> through which you had the power to do so.
>
> Continue your generosity to me,
> so that my soul that you redeemed
> may be freed from my body pleasing to you.[16]

Many men and women in history have known the heights, depths, and freedom of Dante and Beatrice. Consider, for instance, Mary, the mother of Jesus, and Joseph, her husband. Because we tend to think of Joseph as an old man, a father who stands by Mary and protects her as his child, we hardly dare to imagine that Mary and Joseph could have been passionately, wildly, madly, in love with each other. But I think such passion must have existed between them. The reason is simple: eros seeks eros. As solitaries, Mary and Joseph each knew the burning of eros in his or her relationship with God. Such passion cannot be contained. What makes their life together so amazing to me is that they could feel this fierce desire for one another without expressing it genitally. Although they probably expressed their love in physical ways and probably shared the same bed, I really believe (following centuries of Christian tradition) they could have remained virgins.

A crazy idea. Perhaps impossible according to our present-day mentality. Such love was certainly unheard of in the traditional Jewish concept of marriage, with its premium on large families. Yet, for Mary and Joseph, I think such love would have to exist if they were honest with one another. Their love for one another could not overlook or ignore their primary consecration to God. Instead, they creatively embraced this consecration in a conjugal form of celibacy and continence. This could have been the ultimate expression of their love for one another, their supreme sacrifice of each other to God. Certainly, it is not important whether or not Mary and Joseph ever did enjoy sexual intercourse. What is important is that they were able to love chastely; their sexuality did not prevent them from living in total dedication to God.[17] Their love for each other enabled them both to become more authentic, more human, and more religious.

The early Church seems to have had some understanding of such a man-woman relationship. St. Paul was a celibate, but his writings mention his constant female companion(s). Perhaps Paul himself practiced *syneisaktism,* a non-coital, man-woman relationship of intimacy. If not taken from his own personal experience, he does at least write to the Corinthians about such a relationship. *The New English Bible* translation reads:

> If a man has a partner in celibacy and feels that he is not behaving properly toward her, if, that is, his instincts are too strong for him, and something must be done . . . let them marry. But if a man is steadfast in his purpose, being under no compulsion, and has complete control of his own choice; and if he has decided in his own mind to preserve his partner in her virginity, he will do well. Thus, he who marries his partner does well, and he who does not will do better (1 Co. 7:36–38).

In another letter, this time to the Romans, Paul also refers to this type of man-woman relationship.

> I implore you by God's mercy to offer your very selves to him: a living sacrifice, dedicated and fit for his acceptance, the worship offered by mind and heart. Adapt yourselves no longer to the pattern of this present world, but let your minds be remade and your whole nature thus transformed (Rm. 12:1–2).

Various forms of *syneisaktism* existed in the early Church, although each relationship of cohabitation of the sexes was supposedly marked by strict continence. Sherwin Derrick, in *Sexual Relation in Christian Thought,* elaborates:

> Certain of the solitary ascetics of the desert were accompanied each by a female hermit who acted more or less as a maidservant to the holy man; in the ancient Irish Church monks and nuns lived together in monastic establishments; and in towns and cities women shared the dwellings of priests and even of bishops, as housekeepers or spiritual companions.[18]

In some cases, the couple would simply share the same house. In others, they would sleep in the same room, sometimes even sharing the same bed.

Church theologians eventually condemned such practices, not because of any inherent evil, but because the practices tended to exaggerate the dichotomy between "spiritual" and "physical" love, between the soul and the body.[19] I present the possibility of virginal eroticism, not to separate genital and nongenital love, but to once again emphasize their integral connectedness and their polarity. Both the eros which expresses itself in coital union and the eros which refrains from such expression can be of tremendous benefit in interpersonal relationships. I stress the virginal possibilities of erotic physical love because they are so frequently doubted in contemporary society.

Despite prohibitions from the Church, for centuries men and women have continued to experience intimate friendships outside marriage. Such relationships have been recorded between, among others, Martin de Porres and Rose of Lima, Augustine of Hippo and Melania, John Crysostom and Olympias, Vincent de Paul and Louise de Marillae, Bernard of Clairvaux and the Duchess of Lorraine, Philip Neri and Catherine of Reici, Bonifice and Lioba, Jordan of Saxony and Diana d'Andalo. But four couples in particular have greatly impressed me.

The first of these couples is St. Jerome and St. Paula. Jerome, despite his condemnation of the practice of *syneisaktism*[20] had a life-long erotic relationship with Paula. This wealthy widow abandoned everything (including her children) to follow Jerome to Palestine and Egypt. Although their friendship was the source of malicious and scandalous gossip, they remained inseparable companions, working together on the translation of the Bible. When Paula died, Jerome went into a severe depression. Some historians say that when he later died, their bodies were buried next to each other; other historians say they were buried together.

Another couple well known for their love for one another is Clare and Francis of Assisi. Clare was eighteen years old when they met. She too left behind her home and family to follow Francis. Although they lived separately, they remained in constant communication. Francis wrote his famous "Canticle of Brother Sun" while visiting Clare at San Damiano. She recounted her passion, both for Francis and for God, in her own writing: "Dispose of me as you please; I am yours by having given my will to God. It is no longer my own."

A third couple I would like to mention is Teresa of Avila and John of the Cross. Both of these celibates were quite ardent and sensual, as evidenced by their writings. They lived together for six years at the convent in Avila, Teresa serving as prioress there and John as spiritual director and confessor. While they were together, Teresa wrote her intensely passionate *Interior Castle,* and John began writing his amorous *Spiritual Canticle.* At least one of John's biographers recounts that when his superiors told him to leave Avila at the end of six years, he refused to do so, and had to be carried off by force. Teresa was twenty-seven years older than John, but this did not seem to deter the fierceness their love. Indeed, it is inconceivable to me that either John or Teresa could have attained the spiritual heights and intimacy in prayer about which they wrote without their passion for one another.

The fourth couple is Francis de Sales and Jane de Chantal. Their story, though occurring centuries later, is similar to that of Jerome and Paula. Jane, a wealthy widow, left the world to follow Francis, her spiritual director. They lived near one another and were in continual communication. Francis's *Treatise on the Love of God* was written for Jane and her sisters of the Visitation. When he died, she buried his body in the church of her convent at Annecy. Later, she was buried near him.

Today, in a society in which the creative and integrative purposes of genitality are stressed and in which pills and other forms of contraception are made readily available, we hear less about intimate friendships that remain virginal. It is hard to believe that our society is devoid of such men-women friendships. One couple of the twentieth century that *has* publicly acknowledged such virginal love is Catherine de Hueck and Eddie Doherty. Sometime after their marriage, they each took a vow of celibacy. In *Poustinia,* Catherine writes of a love which transcends genitality:

> . . . people don't need a bedroom to make love. One can make love any place, and "making love" does not necessarily mean immediately what people think it means! Making love can mean looking into each other's eyes. It can mean holding hands tightly. It means being aware of each other in the midst of a crowd.[21]

Be assured, I am not advocating that we all take vows of celibacy. Nor am I saying that virginal love is better than coital love. What I am saying is this: intimacy means much more than the physical penetration of a vagina. Eros is *always* more expansive, more liberating, and more fulfilling than libido.

I strongly believe that we need to restore intimacy to its ancient sanctity and pricelessness. We are all called in this age to make love to many others, but in ways that embrace and make holy all that is deeply human. Erotic intimacy moves us past our infatuation with breasts, thighs, and penises. It thrusts us forward into full sexual integration, into real communion and communication. It stops at nothing until we have established a genuinely whole intercourse, and even then, eros keeps on going.

֍ 9. BEYOND CELIBACY

SHOULD I marry or remain single? Should I enter religious life? Should I have intercourse or remain virginal? For most of my life, I have considered these questions with utmost seriousness. Choosing my state in life seemed to be the most important decision I could make. Only recently has my thinking about this changed. I no longer look upon marriage, the single life, or religious life as "vocations." We have only one vocation: to become whole. Marriage, the single life and religious life are life-styles subordinant to this one vocation.

Questions about marriage, about celibacy, about virginity are certainly important, but they are not crucial. To give these questions undue emphasis seems to indicate a misunderstanding of celibacy (religious or lay) and marriage. Celibacy and marriage are not opposed to each other, nor are they two sides of the same coin. And one is not the symbol of the union we will one day share with God whereas the other is the reality of such union. Both states of life are symbols. Celibacy is a symbol of our virginal receptivity to God, our ultimate recognition of him as the primary object of our love. Marriage is a symbol of our covenant relationship with God and of the dying to self necessary to become one with him.

We are not called to celibacy alone or to marriage alone. We are called to both. If we are existentially, physically celibate, we must also become psychologically and spiritually married. If we are existentially married, we must also become psychologically and spiritually celibate. Both of these realities aim toward the same goal: union with God. The asceticism of celibacy must go hand in hand with the gnosis of marriage to reach the fullness of God-intoxication and its resulting giving of self.

Traditional Judaism did not contain this insight. The Jewish culture of two thousand years ago placed so much emphasis on marriage that there was no freedom when it came to "choosing" one's life-style. Everyone was expected to marry. The fact that Jesus chose to remain virginal and celibate seems highly significant to me. By not marrying, Jesus affirms virginity and the single life as valid options in pursuing wholeness. He refutes the myth that we are only half persons if we are not married. He overturns the myth that marriage is better than virginity or celibacy. And he advocates maximum personal freedom, affirming that life-styles should be freely chosen.

Psychologists and mystics both tell us that our experience of God leads us from lower forms of love to higher ones. Celibacy and marriage are not "higher" and "lower" in this schema; they are both vestibules to the spiritual odyssey. The progression of love found in any religious experience passes from libido (lust) to eros (desire for the beloved) to agápe (the love God has for us). The struggle to become authentically human motivates the first trans-formation, from libido to eros. The struggle to become fully divine is the challenge of the second transformation, from eros to agápe. Both celibate and married persons are called to undertake these transformations.

Although he never sins, Jesus, better than anyone, embodies both celibacy and marriage. It is this embodiment and the strug-gle to achieve it which I would call his religious experience. In his journey toward union with God, Jesus is like us in inheriting both the temptations of sin and the guilt of Adam's sin. The author of Hebrews is emphatic about this. "Christ is a high priest . . . feeling our weakness with us; one who has been tempted in every way that we are" (Heb. 4:15). Adam (human-ity) gives in to the temptation to reduce eros to libido, realizes the mistake, and then struggles to regain eros. Jesus, in refusing to submit to this temptation, comes to pure eros and is consequently thrust into agápe. He thus becomes the Messiah and frees us to make the same journey. To understand this religious experience more fully—which I believe is also our religious experience—I would like to explore the temptations of Jesus as they relate to celibacy and marriage. In the final chapter, I will develop more fully this religious experience and describe what I consider to be the progression of Jesus' relationship with God and his understanding of love, the significance of his death and the implications of the resurrection.

As I discussed in Chapter 2, the desert or wilderness symbolizes the place where we can see, hear, and touch God directly. But true wilderness also brings us face to face with our demons. This fact is poignantly presented by Nikos Kazantzakis in his *Last Temptation of Christ.* Here, John the Baptist warns Jesus that although he may find God in the desert, he will also hear more clearly the voice of temptation. "Take care," he says, "Satan is lying in wait for you, his army all in order. . . . He shall fall upon you with all his wildness and all his sweetness. Take care. The desert is full of sweet voices, and death."[1]

Matthew does not tell us that Jesus went to the desert; he says Jesus was led into the wilderness. I think this is significant. Jesus, the celibate, is alone in the wilderness. And yet these words also refer us to the Old Testament marriage imagery of Hosea: "I am going to lure her and lead her out into the wilderness and speak to her heart" (2:14). This imagery suggests there are both celibate and married characteristics in Jesus' evolving interaction with God. Once we are lured to eros, we have further struggles to undergo. To become whole, we must not only become fully human; we must let God speak to our hearts, we must let him make us divine.

According to Matthew's account, Jesus never leaves the wilderness. His entire life is portrayed as the place of meeting God, the time of wrestling with his demons, and the journey into the wilderness of his own soul. Matthew can present Jesus in no other

way. Every good Jew knows that God tests and tries the person he
loves most. "Yahweh reproves the person he loves, as a father
checks a well-loved son" (Pr. 3:11–12). Deuteronomy reminds the
Israelites that "Yahweh your God is training you as a man trains
his child" (8:5). The book of Wisdom says to God: "You tested
them indeed, correcting them like a father" (Ws. 11:9–10). The
temptations of Jesus (as do our temptations) continue throughout
the entire journey to wholeness.

Kazantzakis again shows great insight into the humanness of
Jesus when he describes Jesus' original conception of the desert.
Jesus, like us, would like to think that one successful retreat will
be enough, that God will somehow speak to him, and from that
moment on he will know exactly what it is God wants of him.
Jesus, in the *Last Temptation*, says:

> I shall not leave this threshing-floor . . . unless I hear God's voice. But
> I must hear it clearly, I won't be satisfied with the usual steady hum
> or twittering of thunder; I want him to speak to me clearly, with human
> words, and to tell me what he desires from me and what I can, what
> I must, do. Only then will I get up and leave this threshing-floor to
> return to men, if that is his command, or to die, if that is his will, I'll
> do whatever he wishes, but I must know what it is . . . in God's name![2]

Matthew is particularly careful to tell us that Jesus does not meet
God face to face in this desert. He meets demons and angels, but
not God. He leaves the physical desert, but he can indeed say
with William Yeats, "And in my heart the demons and the gods
wage an eternal battle."[3] Jesus must still discern the "will of
God."

In examining the implications of the wilderness temptations of
Jesus, it is important to remember that we see them in retrospect,
and from the viewpoint of one of Jesus' disciples. Jesus himself,
I think, does not fully realize the implications of these temptations
until his death. As he becomes psychologically and spiritually
mature, his God "grows"; his understanding of the divine and his
relationship with God take on greater depths and new meaning.

Likewise, his self-knowledge—in particular his understanding of celibacy and marriage—also deepens.

The first temptation: The tempter came to him and said: "If you are the Son of God, tell these stones to turn into loaves." But Jesus replied: "Scripture says: You do not live on bread alone but on every word that comes from the mouth of God" (Mt. 4:3–4).

Whenever we are unhappy with our lives, we are tempted to think that a change in life-style will solve all our problems. We suppose that if we could only enter or leave religious life, get married or divorced, then we would live "happily ever after." Once we have embraced a new life-style, we expect no more trials. Such illusions are part of the first temptation of Jesus in the wilderness. Implicit in this temptation is the thought that something, be it intercourse, marriage, or religious vows, is all we need. These things are seen as end points, and we forget that the process of self-actualization still goes on after an "end point" has been reached.

To turn stones into loaves is the temptation to find our fulfillment in one specific time in our lives instead of becoming a whole person, a responsible individual before God. Eros does not end with sex or marriage or virginal intimacy. The erotic urge toward individuation is a continual seduction, an "overwhelming passion that goes beyond the natural measure of love."[4] Gail Sheehy, in *Passages,* cites numerous examples of women who have opted for marriage and children to the detriment of their own development. Although the woman who abandons intellectual pursuits upon marriage is a classic example of this first temptation, she is certainly not the only one who is so tempted. All too often, we settle in where we are and do not risk growth or change. Too easily we forget the words of Teresa: "We must strive all the time to advance [on this human journey], and if we are not advancing we must cherish serious misgivings . . . for love is never idle."[5] Each of us, male or female, religious or lay, who is not consciously striving to become more aware, more creative, more in tune with reality, has fallen into this temptation.

No one life-style is easier than another. No matter what option we choose, we must learn to deal with anxiety, the challenge of changing, and the problems involved in becoming whole. Whatever we do, we must continue to embrace trials and suffering, enter into the darkness of Jonah (see Mt. 12:39–42; 16:4), and wrestle with God as did Jacob (Gn. 32:23–32). We cannot start the process of self-knowledge and then stop. "No one," says Sigmund Freud, "who conjures up . . . those half-tamed demons that inhabit the human breast and seeks to wrestle with them, can expect to come through the struggle unscathed."[6] To become whole, we must go through and beyond eros.

Both celibacy and marriage may foster the illusion that man by himself or woman by herself is incomplete. The temptation of the stone is to think we are only half. The temptor says that stones by themselves are not good enough. On a psychic level, this is the temptation not to cope with the animus or anima, and not to meet the other as a whole person. The temptation of bread is to confine God to a provider role. The temptor tries to keep us in an infantile or immature spirituality, one that maintains a parent-child relationship with another person or with God. In this "Daddy take care of me" stance, we refuse to come to eros, and to undergo the metamorphosis necessary for the lover-beloved relationship with another. Full-blown eros demands maturity. It demands horizontal rather than vertical relationships.

The first temptation is also the temptation to find our fulfillment in something other than God. Whether we are religious, married, or single, it is very easy to seek security in an institution (the church, another person, a job) rather than in God. We can compensate for our need for God by becoming filled with every comfort the material world can offer. Our lives can too easily become a pursuit of the mutual gratification of needs. Needs that are very human, but needs that stop there.

To make it past this temptation, for eros to become agápe, our desire for God must become so strong that it leads us to even greater passion. Jesus, facing this temptation, chooses to continue growing in self-knowledge and in experience of God. His response is a precursor of his eventual yes to passion and suffering on the cross as the fully obedient son and, thus, as the Word of God. His response contains the future choice to place himself on life's altar and enter into its transforming fires.

The second temptation: The devil then took him to the holy city and made him stand on the parapet of the Temple. "If you are the Son of God," he said, "throw yourself down; for Scripture says: He will put you in his angels' charge and they will support you on their hands in case you hurt your foot against a stone." Jesus said to him, "Scripture also says: You must not put the Lord your God to the test" (Mt. 4:5–7).

To "throw yourself down" is to become so preoccupied with our own humanness that spirituality fades into the background. Here, we are tempted to do everything ourselves and then call God in. We are tempted to bring others to ourselves rather than to God. I believe Jesus wrestles with this temptation not once, but many times. The demons are with him as he teaches the people, performs spectacular miracles, and rides into Jerusalem to the jubilant adulation of the crowds. The greatest power of evil which Jesus faces is not exterior; it is that which he finds lurking inside himself. Once again, I find the insight of Kazantzakis magnificent:

"Who are you?" said Jesus to his tempter. "Yourself . . . the hungry lion inside your heart and loins. . . . Do you believe I am Temptation, an emissary of the Sly One, come to mislead you? You brainless hermit, what strength can external temptation have? The fortress is taken only from within. I am the deepest voice of your deepest self. I am the lion within you. You have wrapped yourself in the skin of a lamb to encourage men to approach you, so that you can devour them."[7]

It is the temptation to be a good person without God.

It is also the temptation to use God, to approach him simply to get what we want. In this temptation we limit God to the good things that come our way, and interpret the suffering ("in case you hurt your foot against a stone") as evil. How many times have we read Mt. 7:7–11 with only our own limited ideas of what is good for us? Jesus asks, "Is there a person among you who would give a child a stone when he asked for bread?" We of course answer no. But the irony of the story is that God really does hand his children stones. This temptation to limit God is a form of presumption on our part, a type of overconfidence. God becomes our Linus-blanket: someone who will always be there and who will solve all our problems. The crucified Jesus painfully knows the falsity of this presumption. Religious clichés do not lessen the reality of suffering.

Psalm 91 is an excellent example of the trust we should have in God. The accompanying temptation, however, is to carry this trust too far, to live in a superstitious relationship with God, to refuse to assume personal responsibility for our own salvation. Psalm 91 reads: "You need not fear the terrors of the night, the arrow that flies in the daytime. . . . He covers you with his feathers, and you find shelter underneath his wings. . . . You yourself will remain unscathed" (Ps. 91:5, 4, 7). Jesus will eventually testify to the absurdity of carrying this thinking too far. Even Jesus admits there are certain things God cannot do. If we refuse to respond to him, God is helpless. He can do nothing, while sinners prosper and holy persons are stoned to death (see Mt. 21:35; 22:6; 23:27).

The whole question of celibacy as opposed to marriage reflects this temptation to separate the sacred from the profane, the spiritual from the earthy. Self-righteousness or self-contentment can prevent anyone from pure agápe. There are no sure ways and there are certainly no short-cuts to union with God. Regardless of who we are, we can become too independent, too cocksure of ourselves, too confident that God will always be there to bless our projects.

The second temptation is, in my opinion, the temptation to be too virginal or too married. Physical virginity in itself, or sexual intercourse in itself, does not automatically bring about union with God and more loving involvement with others. To be too virginal is to maintain impenetrable barriers to being opened up and loved by another or by the divine ravisher. To be too married is to refuse to believe that the eternal lover can still teach us something about love that is new and beyond our wildest imaginings.

The third temptation: Next, taking him to a very high mountain, the devil showed him all the kingdoms of the world and their splendor. "I will give you all these," he said, "if you fall at my feet and worship me." Then Jesus replied, "Be off, Satan. For Scripture says: You must worship the Lord your God and serve him alone" (Mt. 4:8–10).

Here, in the last temptation presented by Matthew, a force within us that demands false gods struggles against the power which can transform us into God. It is the struggle between lust and reverence, material aims and spiritual growth, power and weakness. Isaiah tells us that, in one way or another, we are all makers of idols (Is. 44:15–17). To set up a false god is, as Evelyn Underhill describes it, an "inveterate habit of trying to rest in or take seriously, things which are 'less than God.' "[8] Deuteronomy warns us against this tendency. We must "set fire to all the carved images . . . of gods, not coveting the gold and silver that covers them" (Dt. 7:25).

Matthew's Jesus repeatedly insists that we renounce our idols and see them for what they really are. "Do not store up treasures for yourself on earth where moths and woodworms destroy them and thieves can break in and steal" (Mt. 6:19). "Be careful not to parade your good deeds before others to attract their notice" (Mt. 6:1). "It will be hard for a rich person to enter the kingdom of heaven" (Mt. 19:23). If we do not free ourselves from these idols, God will detach us from them himself. We must divorce ourselves from all fictions and half-truths, and free our hearts from all that would possess us (see Mt. 11:18–19).

We make an idol out of marriage or celibacy, I now believe, whenever we stubbornly cling to them as permanent life-styles. I believe strongly in the values of commitment and fidelity, and believe that permanency is an ideal toward which to strive. But when a life-style no longer frees and supports us in the journey toward wholeness, then I believe it is our responsibility to dissolve the marriage or terminate the celibate commitment. Our state in life should always be subordinate to what makes ourselves and the ones we love fully human and fully religious. St. Paul, in his letter to the Corinthians, agrees. If a peaceful, humanizing, and loving life together in marriage is not possible, then the Christian is no longer bound (see 1 Co. 7:12–16). If wholeness is no longer possible in a certain commitment, then we must move on. To make a false god is to love something inordinately.

I hope the Catholic Church will further change its position on divorce and remarriage along with its attitudes toward ex-priests and ex-religious persons. Leaving the priesthood or religious life, dissolving a marriage, are indeed traumatic choices, but they may be among the most honest, most Christian, and most growth-producing things a person can do. To penalize or ostracize persons who have carefully thought through such a change in their life-style is, in my opinion, completely contrary to the message of Jesus. We have made something artificial into a god.

Honest discernment is, however, always difficult. Our biggest false god is usually ourselves. It is extremely hard to put aside the *ignes fatui* of our society, to abandon our self-aggrandizing endeavors. It is even harder to let go of the good things we value and the sacred ideals we uphold. "The desert is not big enough for two," says Kazantzakis.[9] Either we live and God "dies," or we die and he lives. Full erotic passion always "carries with it the threat of annihilation of everything."[10] According to Kierkegaard, erotic passion is to will one thing so passionately that we sacrifice everything to achieve it. As John of the Cross says, "I cry for Thee and loose myself from all things that I may cling to Thee."[11] Through eros, we dare to abandon ourselves forever and to leap from our present securities toward deeper experience. We dare to give ourselves away, reserving nothing.

To arrive at union with God, we must, as the ancient alchemists would say, hunt the Green Lion within us. The Green Lion is the demonic, the power which can take over our whole selves. If we repress or ignore the Green Lion, we will be consumed with a thousand false gods and illusions. If we integrate this Lion, take him into ourselves, we will find ourselves transfigured. Says Evelyn Underhill:

It is not by the education of the Lamb, but by the hunting and taming of the wild intractable lion, instinct with vitality, full of ardour and courage, exhibiting heroic qualities on the sensual plane, that the Great Work is achieved. . . . The Green Lion, then, in his strength and wholeness is the only creature potentially able to attain Perfection. It needs the adoption and purification of all the wealth and resources of [our] nature, not merely the encouragement of [our] transcendental tastes, if [we] are to "overtake the Sun" and achieve the Great Work. The kingdom of Heaven is taken by violence, not by amiable aspiration. "The Green Lion," says one alchemist, "is the priest by whom Sol and Luna are wed." In other words, the raw stuff of indomitable human nature is the means by which [we are] to attain union with the Absolute.[12]

There is a catch to the alchemist's story, however. To tame the Green Lion, to really integrate him, we must behead him. And because he is a part of ourselves, we too must die. Only then will the Green Lion become the Red Dragon. Only then will the human become divine, eros become agápe.

Celibacy as a vocational life-style can be a potent symbol of such dying. For, as I mentioned in Chapter 3, celibacy reminds us of our finiteness, of the fact that we will not live forever. Celibates (both religious and lay) can give into the third temptation by attempting to perpetuate themselves through numerous achievements, writings, projects, or students. Marriage, as the fusion of two separate identities into one, can also be a rich symbol of death. We have obscured this symbolism by traditionally associating intercourse with procreation. Although use of today's contraceptives makes the death symbolism of sex more apparent, this too can contribute to the seductions of the third temptation. Sex can deny death by becoming a life-sustainer; coitus can become a proof and measure of the amount of youthful vitality we have within us.

It is no small wonder to me that Jesus is disgusted when the Pharisees ask him about the status of marriage and celibacy in heaven (see Mt. 22:23–29). They have distorted the importance of these life-styles. Jesus tells the Pharisees that heaven is the immersion of a person so intimately in God, that "men and women are like angels" (Mt. 22:30). This does not mean that we will be asexual in heaven; it simply means that the experience of God will be so powerful that both virginity and nonvirginity will become irrelevant.

The meaning of the third temptation is the challenge to die, to stand still long enough to embrace the full impact of eros, and in so doing, to open ourselves up to greater faith. Only in this leap of faith, can we surrender ourselves fully like Jesus. Only then do we cease to be our own barrier to the divine. When we can rid ourselves of all that encumbers us, we can be made whole. When we can allow ourselves to become so vulnerable that we are as nothing, God rushes in. "Now he takes over, and that's where true liberation begins."[13] The fullness of celibate passion, the sharing of God's own passion, can then lead us beyond marriage and beyond celibacy.

❦ 10. BELOVED CHILD

CELIBATE passion is a journey. Anyone today who would set off on this adventure is advised to find a spiritual director, someone who will be a guiding light through the darkness and confusion of inner consciousness. This is not new advice; it is the wisdom of all ages and all cultures. Progress in the spiritual life has always been associated with such guides: the Hindu guru, the Buddhist master, the Russian staretz, the Jewish rabbi, the Catholic novice director, the Sufi shaikh, and many others. If we would seek union with God, we must have some constant companion who can make us aware of the truth and who can lead us to transcend ourselves. For, as Ghazahli says, "the way of the faith is obscure, but the devil's ways are many and patent, and he who has no shaikh to guide him will be led by the devil into his ways."[1] Both John of the Cross and Teresa of Avila are adamant about the necessity for a good director.

We usually think of Jesus as a spiritual master who lives for three years with twelve disciples. But the Jesus portrayed by Matthew is a seeker all the way to Mount Golgotha. This leads me to believe that although Jesus is a teacher of others, he still needs someone to help him face his ever-growing relationship with God. If the religious experience of Jesus is really the same as ours, then who was his spiritual master? The Gospels never tell us directly, but they do provide hints. John the Baptist is probably one of the most influential teachers in Jesus' life, but none of the Gospels indicate a long-term relationship between him and Jesus. It seems to me that there is only one person who could know Jesus well enough to really guide him through the human to the divine. That person, I believe, is his mother.

This realization has surprised and delighted me. For some reason (perhaps cultural), I had never even considered the possibility. I realize now that Mary is no ordinary woman; her spirituality is not pietistic or superficial. She is not a pray-er of prayers; she really prays. She is a contemplative who, by the time she is fifteen, knows not only the prayer of quiet but the full intensity of celibate passion, the prayer of union. St. Luke's description of the Annunciation compares strikingly with that of a person in Teresa's fifth or sixth mansion who has become so emptied that God's inseminating onrush is inevitable. Suddenly, in kenotic ecstasy, Mary is lifted beyond all the limitations of celibacy and of marriage to enter into total and complete union with God.[2]

Mary is no beginner in the spiritual life. She is St. Teresa's "proficient *par excellence*" who knows God directly. I once thought that when Luke describes her as one who "pondered these things in her heart," he meant that she is ignorant and does not understand what is happening. I now think this phrase means that Mary is one who experiences God so exquisitely that she treasures all things as his gift and is continually filled with wonder at his surprising manifestations.

Matthew tells us nothing of the private life of Jesus. It is quite possible that Jesus spent most of these thirty years with his mother. Some psychologists might criticize this theory, saying that Jesus appears overly dependent on his mother and is led into the desert at thirty years of age to come to terms with his demonic anima. In this theory, I prefer to think that Jesus recognizes his mother as a person who experiences God, and thus chooses to dwell near her, as a disciple would choose to live with his or her director.

Although Jesus leaves his mother, it seems likely that he periodically returns to her (consider Mt. 4:13; 8:5; 9:1; 12:46; 13:1, 54). Mary is with him to the end, even to the cross. She is for Jesus what Beatrice is for Dante, a guide into the mysteries of love itself. In his Gospel, Matthew carefully lays out the progression of love which Jesus learns. First he learns what it means to love as a son. Gradually, as he is weaned from childhood dependency (both physical and spiritual), he learns what it means to be a lover. This learning is not an intellectual "head trip"; it is an experiential journey into deeper relationship, both with God and with Mary.

The first direct contact Jesus has with God is his hearing of an inner voice say, "This is my Son, the Beloved" (Mt. 3:17). Matthew cleverly indicates that the first two wilderness temptations hinge on the condition "if you are the Son of God" (4:3, 6). The first major struggle in the spiritual journey of Jesus is to understand and realize the meaning of being a son. The forty-day struggle in the wilderness appears to be a struggle between Jesus and his concept of God as father. Every time Matthew employs the phrase "Son of God," he refers to the original temptations. It is important to note that Matthew's Jesus never calls himself the "Son of God"; it is always another person or a personified demon who taunts him with this phrase.

There are five places in Matthew's Gospel where the phrase "Son of God" occurs. In chapter 8, two demons scream at Jesus: "What do you want with us, Son of God? Have you come here to torture us before the time?" (8:28–34). Later on, his own disciples bow down before Jesus and say, "Truly you are the Son of God" (14:33). Twice, Peter is the demonic voice of temptation. When Jesus asks him who he thinks he is, Peter replies, "You are the Christ, the Son of the living God" (16:16). At the transfiguration, Peter says, "I will make three tents here, one for you, one for Moses, and one for Elijah" (17:14). Pilate also puts before Jesus the temptation, "Tell us if you are the Christ, the Son of God" (26:63). Each time Jesus is confronted by this phrase, his concept of sonship as it relates to God assumes new and more significant meaning.

Jesus does not come to any clear-cut answer after forty days in the desert. He returns home to his mother to struggle anew with the concept of being a son. Perhaps because he is not certain about his identity, he is content to continue the work of John the Baptist.

Matthew says that Jesus begins his preaching with the very same message of John: "Repent, for the kingdom of heaven is close at hand" (4:17; 3:2). John's Gospel tells us that it is not until later, at the wedding of Cana, that Mary pushes Jesus to take more initiative. He thinks he is not ready; Mary, who knows otherwise, insists, and directs Jesus to transcend his poor self-concept (see Jn. 2:1–12).

Beginning with chapter 5 of Matthew's Gospel, we find a Jesus who attempts to grapple with the relation between son and father. His message now is new. The father of the Israelites is not David or even Abraham; it is God. Jesus teaches his followers to pray using the words "our Father" (6:9). However, careful scrutiny of Matthew's text shows us that Jesus' idea of father is very much influenced by a Jewish concept emphasizing fear of the father. This concept of the feared father is reflected in Jesus' Sermon on the Mount. This sermon seems to me to have been an explanation of several Old Testament psalms. God is presented as a father who is a just judge, a lawgiver, a rewarder of good, and a punisher of evil. Here are excerpts of the psalms and Jesus' explanations of them:

GOD AS JUST: The wicked will be expelled, while those who hope in Yahweh shall have the land for their own. . . . A little longer, and the wicked will be no more. . . . The arms of the wicked are doomed to break, and Yahweh will uphold the virtuous (Ps. 37:9, 10, 16).

Happy the gentle, they shall have the earth for their heritage. . . . Happy those who are persecuted in the cause of right; theirs is the kingdom of heaven (Mt. 5:4, 10).

GOD AS GOOD: Trust in Yahweh and he will give you what your heart desires. . . . Yahweh takes care of the good. . . . They will not be at a loss when bad times come. In time of famine they will have more than they need. . . . I never saw a virtuous person deserted, . . . for Yahweh supports him by the hand (Ps. 37:3, 4, 18, 19, 25, 24).

Happy the poor in spirit; theirs is the kingdom of heaven. . . . Happy those who hunger and thirst for what is right; they shall be satisfied (Mt. 5: 3, 6).

GOD AS REWARDER: The angel of Yahweh pitches camp around those who fear him; and he keeps them safe. . . . The face of Yahweh frowns on evil persons. . . . His eyes are turned toward the virtuous. . . . They cry for help and Yahweh hears and rescues them from all their troubles (Ps. 34: 7, 9, 16, 17).

Happy those who mourn; they shall be comforted. . . . Happy the pure of heart; they shall see God (Mt. 5: 5, 8).

In Matthew's Gospel, the concept of God as just judge continues throughout Jesus' early teachings. We who would be good children to this Father must keep the law both with others and in our hearts (5:17-20). To be a child means to listen to the Father and to act upon his words (7:21-24). God is the rewarder who brings happiness and good things to the virtuous (7:20; 12:33; 13:30); his forgiveness is always conditional (6:14-15; 7:1).

An important change in Jesus' thought and experience of God is reflected in Matthew's chapter 8. Jesus returns to Capernaum, and most likely, to Mary (8:5). I can almost hear her suggesting to Jesus that his understanding of the parent-child relationship is too limited. There is more to his relationship with God than Jesus has yet realized. At precisely this time in Matthew's account, two demons confront Jesus again with the mysterious words "Son of God." Jesus wrestles anew with these words, and moves toward a deeper understanding of God. Matthew's Jesus now stresses the importance of leaving behind parental security and of breaking down notions which equate the God-person relationship with keeping the law.

Jesus now preaches that people who would seek union with God cannot rest in any security (8:20). We cannot be content to approach God as dutiful children (8:22). If we prefer to remain in the safe, warm womb, we will never be able to grow or mature (10:37-39). If we are not always doing violence to our limited concepts of God, we will never find the courage to surpass and transcend them in a more significant relationship (10:34-36). The moment we become sure of who God is, of what this Father means, we close ourselves off to further possibilities. Refusal to grow is refusal to be and to become a true child of God (12:46–50).

Jesus expresses his new understanding of the Father not only in his words but in his actions. No longer is Jesus concerned about keeping the letter of the law. Instead, he transcends the literal to live by its spirit. Matthew tells us that the new Jesus eats with tax collectors and sinners (9: 10–13) and does not fast (9:14–15). He violates the rigid demands of the Sabbath by walking too far, eating when hungry (12:1–8), and by performing miracles (12:-9–13). No longer does he keep the traditions of the elders (15:1–9).

At this time in his life, Jesus begins to grapple with the meaning of "Beloved." He stresses renunciation of all former idols because he desires something more in his relationship with God. He begins to long for a God that is bigger than his previous conceptions. Here, I perceive the clear emergence of eros in Jesus. It leads him to a new concept of Father as the compassionate one, and it forces him to see God as the eternal lover. At this critical time, Matthew's Jesus stays close to Capernaum (see Mt. 9:1; 12:46; 13:1, 54). He is in need of someone to help him through his inner turmoil, and to me, it is quite logical that he would turn to Mary, who has already experienced God as lover.

When Matthew tells us that Jesus calls a tax collector to be a disciple and eats with sinners (9:9–10), he is also commenting on eros. Eros always expresses itself in the desire to share, to make whole, to heal, to have compassion. Twice, Jesus says that his new God wants mercy instead of sacrifice (9:13; 12:7). This God does not want our exterior actions, nor does he judge us solely on our behavior. He wants our love; God wants to know us, despite our mistakes and undesirableness. Jesus goes so far as to suggest that God is the bridegroom who wants to live with us. The purpose of fasting, asceticism, and exterior ritual is to entice this bridegroom closer. Once he has come, once we are enjoying his presence, there is no need to fast (9:14–15). It is absurd to act as if God were far distant, and thus perpetuate the preparations for his coming, when in fact he is already with us.

Jesus' growing experience of eros in his spiritual journey manifests itself in two further ways. First, Jesus himself becomes more compassionate. It is not until chapter 9 of Matthew's Gospel that we find an expressly empathetic Jesus. Matthew now says, "He felt sorry for the crowds" (9:36). "He saw a large crowd and he took pity on them and healed their sick" (14:14). "I feel sorry for these people" (15:32). "Jesus felt pity for them" (20:34). Jesus becomes more aware of the simple things in life, and now cherishes the foolish, the useless, and the childish (18:1–4, 5–7; 19:13–15). Like his mother, he now treasures all things and approaches the grandeurs and absurdities of life with profound wonder.

Second, Jesus grows in his desire to please God, now no longer motivated by fear but by love. He serves the crowds, overlooking his own needs (14:13–14) and becomes Isaiah's suffering servant (12:18–21). More than ever, he desires to do the will of the Father (26:42), even if it means suffering and death (12:38–42; 17:12, 22–23).

Chapter 17 of Matthew's Gospel contains the account of the transfiguration. Again Jesus hears the haunting words, "Behold my Son, my Beloved" (17:5). I believe this is another turning point in the spiritual life of Jesus. Although he never fully understands the meaning of "Son," he is now called to experience the meaning of "Beloved." I believe that on this mountain of transfiguration Jesus first tastes God as lover. Eros erupts into union, and Jesus will never again be the same.

Just preceding the transfiguration, Jesus tells his disciples, "If you want to be a follower of mine, renounce yourself, take up your cross, and follow me" (16:24). These words are affirmed on the mountaintop. We cannot see God and live. God alone. So strong is eros within Jesus that his sense of death becomes acute. Jesus now speaks in terms of total renunciation and inevitable annihilation. "The Son of Man will suffer" (17:12). "They will put him to death" (17:22–23). "They will condemn him to death and will hand him over to the pagans to be mocked and scourged and crucified" (20:17–19). "The Son of Man will be handed over to be crucified" (26:1).

An intense awareness of the necessity for vigilance now grips Jesus. He speaks of the last days (24:26–31) and of the need to be consciously alert to the Master's coming (24:45). He tells us that God himself is the bridegroom, that we must be wise virgins who are ready for him (25:1–13). All of our resources, talents, and dreams must be spent out of an increasing desire to please God (25:14–30). Jesus is not joking when he says to "go and sell what you own and give the money to the poor" (19:21). His very body is sold and the money given to buy a potter's field (27:6–10).

Rainer Maria Rilke once wrote in a letter, "If my devils are to leave me, I am afraid my angels will take flight as well."[3] Through his imagery, Matthew shows that this statement applies as well to Jesus. His angels and demons harrass him all the way to death. The demonic, as Rollo May points out, is a potential power for active loving. "To be able to experience and live out capacities for tender love requires the confronting of the daimonic."[4] The demon, according to Plato, is our bond with the divine. Only the integrated demon pushes us to greater relatedness.

Perhaps this is the meaning of bearing one's cross. No human person can ever become pure enough to merit the divine attention, let alone deserve the overtures of God's love. The reality of human unworthiness is present in Matthew's Jesus. He bears the weight of humanity's sin, and he knows the effects of evil, both subjectively and objectively. Slowly, Jesus realizes that we cannot expel evil in this life. Our demons and their possibility for good and evil will always be with us.

We find this new consciousness in Jesus beginning with Matthew's chapter 12. Jesus says here, "Every kingdom divided against itself is heading for ruin; and no town, no household divided against itself can stand" (12:25). After a moment's reflection upon this, we painfully realize our own incapacity to be undivided. Jesus knows this division within himself, although he does not let it master him. This is essential to the spirituality of Jesus. We must face the Green Lion and tame him, or this demon "will go off and collect seven other spirits more evil than itself" (12:43).

To tame the Green Lion does not mean to get rid of him. For

indeed, our angels will leave us as well. "Do not weed out the bad, because when you weed out the darnel, you might pull up the wheat with it" (13:29). We must take our demons with us to death; meanwhile, we must integrate them into our beings, so that when we offer ourselves to the other in death, we may bring our whole selves, both dark and light sides.

To accept one's own evil is the hardest cross of all to bear. And this, I believe, is the essential kenosis of Jesus. As he is in the throes of death, he does not know if everything in his life has been fraudulent or not. On the cross God is not there. If Jesus has been the upright person, then everything he has believed about God has been a lie. Yahweh does not uphold the virtuous. He does let us fail. He does desert the devout. The evildoers are not punished. If, however, everything Jesus has believed about God is true, then he must himself be wicked, unfaithful, and evil to deserve such punishment. Perhaps to allude to this struggle, Matthew presents to us a Jesus who is very much like the prostitute. His description of the passion and death of Jesus is too analogous to Hosea's description of the unfaithful wife to overlook:

Hosea	*Matthew*
Because his wife has played the whore and has run after false gods, he will punish her. "I will strip her naked . . . turn her into arid land and leave her to die of thirst." (2:3)	"Then they stripped him," (27:28) "They gave him wine to drink mixed with gall, which he tasted but refused to drink." (27:34)
"I mean to withdraw my corn and my wine." (2:9)	"I will not drink wine until the day I drink the new wine with you in the kingdom of my Father." (26:29)
"I will retrieve my wool, my flax, that were intended to cover her nakedness." (2:9)	"They took off the cloak and dressed him in his own clothes." (27:31) "They shared out his clothing by casting lots." (27:35)

Hosea	*Matthew*
"So I will display her shame before her lovers' eyes and no one shall rescue her from my power." (2:10)	"They collected the whole cohort around him . . . to make fun of him." (27:28–29) "Save yourself. If you are God's Son, come down from the cross." (27:39–40)[5]
"I will put an end to her rejoicing, her feasts, her new moons, her Sabbaths and all her solemn festivals." (2:11)	The crucifixion occurs between the Passover festival and the Sabbath. (27:62; 28:1)
"I am going to block her way with thorns." (2:8)	"Having twisted some thorns into a crown, they put this on his head." (27:29)
"She decked herself with rings and necklaces." (2:13)	"They made him wear a scarlet cloak." (27:29–31)
"I will make her sleep secure. I will betroth her to myself forever." (2:19)	"Jesus, again crying out in a loud voice, yielded up his spirit." (27:50)

Matthew further tells us that at the death of Jesus, the veil of the Temple is torn from top to bottom (27:51). In the Old Testament, it is only the prostitute who is veiled. Jesus' body is sold for thirty pieces of silver (26:15) and he is betrayed by a kiss (26:50), both smacking of the prostitute analogy.

Upon further reflection, it seems to me that in using this analogy, Matthew presents to us a crucified Jesus who is the archetype of wholeness. He personifies the struggle to reconcile all opposites: son and lover, virgin and whore, virtue and evil, human and divine. For this reason, Matthew must present to us the side of Jesus we seldom think about. Jesus on the cross embodies the whole unfaithful nation of Israel presenting itself before Yahweh. He takes with him to this death-marriage both good and evil, angels and devils, innocence and guilt. And thus, as John of the Cross says:

He wrought herein the greatest work that He had ever wrought . . . which was the reconciliation and union of mankind, through grace, with God. And this . . . was the moment and the time when this Lord was most completely annihilated in everything. Annihilated . . . with respect to human reputation, since, when men saw Him die, they mocked Him rather than esteemed Him, and also with respect to nature, since His nature was annihilated when he died; and further with respect to the spiritual consolation and protection of the Father, since at that time He forsook Him, that He might pay the whole of man's debt and unite him with God, being thus annihilated and reduced as it were to nothing.[6]

In the moment of death, Jesus lets go of everything. Eros becomes so strong that union is inevitable. Because Jesus has become so empty, so reduced to nothing, God rushes in. Jesus transcends all boundaries. He is no longer Son but Beloved. He is not the bridegroom but the bride. Virgin and yet faithless wife, eros and yet tempted by libido. The overwhelming surprise of the cross is that God can love what is unlovable and ugly. In the moment of union, eros becomes pure agápe. The human becomes divine. Jesus becomes the Christ, the Son of God, the Beloved. Hosea resounds with this discovery: "I will betroth you to myself with faithfulness and you will come to know Yahweh. . . . I will love Unloved; I will say to No-People-of-Mine, 'You are my people' " (2:22, 24).

The intensity of erotic love (Spirit) between Jesus and God reaches such a pitch on the cross that a creative and emancipating climax is inevitable. The intimate exhilaration of total absorption in the Beloved overcomes and destroys any former feelings of separateness. God teaches Jesus on the cross the meaning of a completely new way of loving. As God penetrates the human, we become intimate with everything. "The soul seems to be God rather than a soul and is indeed God by participation."[7] Thus, death becomes the moment of conception, of birth, and of rebirth.

When eros becomes agápe, it becomes miraculously creative. It cannot be contained. Death is changed to new life. God sows his seed and brings forth his own child. Hosea and Matthew confirm this discovery: "I will sow him in the country; I will love Unloved" (Hos. 2:25). Jesus becomes the seed of God which God places in the womb-tomb of the earth (Mt. 27:57–61). New progeny arise. "In the place where they were told, 'You are no people of mine,'" they will be called 'the sons of the living God' "(Ho. 2:2). The miracle foretold by John the Baptist has come true. God has raised up children from stones. When Matthew tells us that after Jesus' death "rocks were split, tombs opened, and the bodies of many rose from the dead" (Mt. 27:52), he means precisely this. God has created his own children. Jesus becomes the Christ (Mt. 28:3). Once again the miracle of the Annunciation has occurred. The soul takes flight in adoration and praise, in communion with God, and a child is born.

Just what does the Christ-event really mean? What difference does Jesus make? I suspect that the answers to these questions will continue to evolve as I grow older, but for now my answer is a simple one. So simple and yet so profound. Jesus, a human being, someone like me, has become God's beloved child. So too, each of us has the same capacity to become the son or daughter of God. To be fully human is to become fully divine. This, to me, is the meaning of life and what celibate passion is all about. This is the journey we each must travel from libido through eros to agápe. Each of us can become the Christ, the child, the beloved. Each of us has the capacity to raise up new children for God.

There seems to be a secret to this transformation; and that is where Jesus comes in. The only way any of us can become divine is by entering into a total and irrevocable transformation. To bring to birth God's child requires, as Teresa says, a total commitment on our part, a tremendous singlehearted passion. Only then will we not fail "to draw the Almighty to become one with our lowliness and to transform us into himself and to effect a union between Creator and the creature."[8] If I long for God enough, desire him with every movement of my being, he will reveal himself to me wholly. If I become fully myself, uniquely celibate and intensely passionate, God will penetrate me completely and make me divine.

Celibate passion can never be a selfish endeavor or a private enterprise. Now more than ever, I believe that what I do in solitude, what I do as one individual—how much I allow God to enter and work through me—will have cosmic consequences. Ish will wed Esh; fire and earth will be one. Eros will ignite more passion. From nothing, we will all rise and become alive. Each of us will burn and be grounded; each of us will become God's beloved, God's child.

NOTES

1. MULTIPLE ONENESS

1. Abraham Heschel, *Man is Not Alone* (New York: Farrar, Straus & Young, 1951), p. 30.
2. Anne Morrow Lindbergh, *Gift from the Sea* (New York: Random House, 1955), pp. 6–7.
3. Kahlil Gibran, *The Prophet* (New York: Alfred A. Knopf, 1951), pp. 15–16.
4. Pierre Teilhard de Chardin, *How I Believe*, trans. Rene Hague (New York: Harper & Row, 1969), p. 53.
5. Alan Watts, *The Two Hands of God* (New York: Macmillan, 1963), p. 48.
6. Lao Tzu, "Poem 42," *The Way of Life*, trans. R. B. Blakney (New York: New American Library, 1955), p. 95.
7. Cornelia Jessey, "Not Yin and Yang, but Ish and Esh," *Way* 28, no. 4 (1972): 15–19.
8. Heschel, *Man is Not Alone*, p. 61.
9. Nicholas of Cusa, *The Vision of God*, trans. Emma Gurney Salter (New York: E. P. Dutton, 1928).
10. *Mandukya Upanishad*, chapter 7, quoted in Sarvepalli Radhakrishnan and Charles A. Moore, eds., *A Sourcebook in Indian Philosophy* (Princeton: Princeton University Press, 1957), p. 56.
11. D. T. Suzuki, *Zen Buddhism*, ed. William Barrett (Garden City, N.Y.: Doubleday, 1956), p. 84.
12. *Ibid.*, p. 10.
13. Hermann Hesse, *Siddhartha* (New York: New Directions, 1951), p. 106.

2. DESERT GARDEN

1. Catherine Doherty, *Poustinia: Christian Spirituality of the East for Western Man* (Notre Dame: Ave Maria Press, 1973), p. 42.

3. FLAMING PHOENIX

1. D. H. Lawrence, "The Phoenix," in *The Complete Poems of D. H. Lawrence,* ed. Vivian de Sola Pinto and F. Warren Roberts (New York: Viking, 1964).
2. Teilhard de Chardin, *How I Believe,* p. 36.
3. Michael Novak, *The Experience of Nothingness* (New York: Harper & Row, 1971), p. 12.
4. St. Catherine of Siena, *The Dialogue of St. Catherine of Siena,* trans. Algar Thorold (Rockford, Ill: Tan Books and Publishers, 1974), p. 274.
5. See Martin Heidegger, *Being and Time,* trans. John Macquarrie and Edward Robinson (New York: Harper & Row, 1962), Pt. II.
6. St. John of the Cross, *Ascent of Mount Carmel,* trans. E. Allison Peers (Garden City, N.Y.: Doubleday, Image Books, 1958), p. 156.
7. St. John of the Cross, *Dark Night of the Soul,* trans. E. Allison Peers (Garden City, N.Y.: Doubleday, Image Books, 1959), p. 106.
8. Nikos Kazantzakis, *Report to Greco* (New York: Simon & Schuster, 1965), p. 247.
9. St. John of the Cross, *Dark Night,* p. 100.
10. Søren Kierkegaard, *Sickness unto Death* and *Fear and Trembling,* trans. Walter Lowrie (Garden City, N.Y. Doubleday, Anchor Books, 1954), p. 181.
11. Søren Kierkegaard, *The Concept of Dread,* trans. Walter Lowrie (Princeton: Princeton University Press, 1957), p. 110.
12. Ernest Becker, *The Denial of Death* (New York: Free Press, 1973), p. 73.
13. *Ibid.,* p. 55.
14. See Raymond A. Moody, Jr., *Life After Life* (New York: Bantam Books, 1975); Elizabeth Kubler-Ross, *On Death and Dying* (New York: Macmillan, 1969); *Questions and Answers on Death and Dying* (New York: Macmillan, 1974); *Death: The Final Stage of Growth* (Englewood Cliffs, N.J.: Prentice-Hall, 1975); *Images of Growth and Death* (Englewood Cliffs, N.J.: Prentice-Hall, 1976).
15. *The Tibetan Book of the Dead,* trans. Francesca Fremantle and Chogyam Trungpa (Boulder, Col.: Shambhala, 1975), pp. 37, 99.

4. MIDNIGHT SUN

1. St. Teresa of Avila, *Interior Castle,* trans. E. Allison Peers (Garden City, N.Y.: Doubleday 1961), p. 185.
2. C. S. Lewis, *The Lion, The Witch, and The Wardrobe* (New York: Macmillan, 1950), p. 149.
3. Teresa of Avila, *Interior Castle,* p. 146.
4. Richard of St. Victor, "De Quatuor Gradibus Violentae Charitatis," paraphrased by Evelyn Underhill, *Mysticism* (New York: World, 1955), p. 379.
5. Kabir, *The Poems of Kabir,* trans. Rabindranath Tagore (Calcutta: Macmillan, 1970), p. 40.
6. Teresa of Avila, *Interior Castle,* p. 131.
7. St. John of the Cross, *Dark Night of the Soul,* pp. 104–5.
8. Underhill, *Mysticism,* p. 388.

9. Rabindranath Tagore, *Fireflies* (New York: Macmillan, 1928), p. 206.
10. See St. John of the Cross, *Living Flame of Love,* trans. E. Allison Peers (New York: Doubleday, Image Books, 1962), p. 55.
11. See St. John of the Cross, *Ascent of Mount Carmel,* p. 107.
12. See Becker, *The Denial of Death,* p. 174.
13. Underhill, *Mysticism,* p. 388.
14. Nikos Kazantzakis, *St. Francis* (New York: Ballantine Books, 1966), p. 20.
15. Thomas Merton, *The Climate of Monastic Prayer* (Spencer, Mass.: Cistercian Publications, 1969), p. 121.
16. Kazantzakis, *Report to Greco,* p. 497.
17. Maurice Maeterlinck, Introduction to John Ruysbroeck, *Adornment of the Spiritual Marriage,* as quoted in F. C. Happold, *Mysticism: A Study and An Anthology* (Baltimore: Penguin Books, 1963), p. 88.

5. BURNING GROUND

1. John Ruysbroeck, *The Book of the Twelve Beguines,* trans. J. Francis (London, 1913), chap. 10.
2. St. Augustine, *Confessions,* trans. Edward B. Pusey (New York: Washington Square Press, 1951), p. 177.
3. Suzuki, *Zen Buddhism,* p. 83.
4. Carl Gustav Jung, *Psyche and Symbol,* ed. Violet S. de Laszlo (Garden City, N.Y.: Doubleday, 1958), p. 332.
5. Bengali Hymn, quoted in Huston Smith, *The Religions of Man* (New York: Harper & Row, 1958), p. 84.

6. IMPASSIONED PRESENCE

1. Walter Kerr, *The Decline of Pleasure* (New York: Simon & Schuster, 1962), p. 137.
2. Robert Neale, *In Praise of Play* (New York: Harper & Row, 1969), p. 82.
3. *Ibid.,* p. 84.
4. *Ibid.,* p. 97.
5. Abraham Heschel, *The Sabbath* (New York: World, 1951), p. 1.
6. Jung, *Psyche and Symbol,* p. 128.
7. William McNamara, "The Meaning of Festivity," *Desert Call,* Special Anniversary Issue (May, 1971): 50.
8. T. S. Eliot, "Little Gidding," *Four Quartets* (New York: Harcourt, Brace & World, 1943), p. 59.
9. Kerr, *Decline of Pleasure,* p. 207.
10. St. Teresa of Avila, *Interior Castle,* p. 223.
11. Nikos Kazantzakis, *Zorba the Greek* (New York: Simon & Schuster, 1952), p. 273.
12. Gerardus Van der Leeuw, *Sacred and Profane Beauty: The Holy in Art,* trans. David E. Green (New York: Holt, Rinehart, & Winston, 1963), p. 29.

13. Dante Alighieri, *The Divine Comedy*, trans. H. R. Huse (New York: Rinehart, 1958). Dante writes of the dance of the fiery spirits (Paradise, canto VII, line 4), of the lofty Seraphim (Paradise, canto VIII, line 25), of the blazing stars —who seem "to be ladies not ending a dance but silently waiting and listening until they have heard the new measure"—(Paradise, canto X, lines 75–80), and of the Principalities and Archangels (Paradise, canto XXVIII, lines 124–25).

14. *Ibid.*, Paradise, canto XII, lines 22–24.

15. Heschel, *The Sabbath*, p. 100.

7. CELIBATE PASSION

1. St. John of the Cross, *Dark Night of the Soul*, p. 133.

2. Rollo May, *Love and Will* (New York: Dell, 1969), pp. 73–74.

3. Anthony Kosnik et al., *Human Sexuality: New Directions in American Catholic Thought* (New York: Paulist Press, 1977), p. 164.

4. Erich Neumann, *Amor and Psyche: The Psychic Development of the Feminine* (Princeton: Princeton University Press, 1971), p. 84.

5. William McNamara, "Love Story or Death Rattle," *Desert Call* (Fall, 1971): 3–4.

6. Rainer Maria Rilke, quoted in Anna Morrow Lindbergh, *Gift from the Sea*, p. 94.

7. St. Teresa of Avila, *The Way of Perfection*, trans. E. Allison Peers (Garden City, N.Y.: Doubleday, 1964), pp. 70–71.

8. William Johnston, *Silent Music: The Science of Meditation* (New York: Harper & Row, 1974), p. 153.

9. Erich Fromm, *The Art of Loving* (New York: Harper & Row, 1962), p. 112.

10. Irene Claremont de Castillejo, *Knowing Woman: A Feminine Psychology* (New York: Harper & Row, 1973), p. 21.

11. Martin Semple, "Chastity and Celibacy: Chastity in Contemporary Moral Theology," *Sisters Today* (June/July, 1972), p. 591.

12. McNamara, "Love Story," p. 2.

13. May, *Love and Will*, p. 64.

14. An example of this thinking may be found in the following passage: "Even the smallest degree of incomplete venereal pleasure has reference by its very nature to legitimate sexual intercourse and to that alone. . . . It is grievously sinful in the unmarried deliberately to procure or to accept even the smallest degree of true venereal pleasure; secondly, it is equally sinful to think, say, or do anything with intention of arousing even the smallest degree of this pleasure." Henry Davis, *Moral and Pastoral Theology* (London: Sheed & Ward, 1936), 2: 180–82.

15. Alan Watts, *Nature, Man and Woman* (New York: Pantheon Books, 1958), pp. 196–201, passim.

16. Morton Hunt, *The Natural History of Love* (New York: Alfred A. Knopf, 1959), p. 55.

17. Herbert W. Richardson, *Nun, Witch, Playmate: The Americanization of Sex* (New York: Harper & Row, 1971), p. 55.
18. Lindbergh, *Gift from the Sea,* p. 104.
19. Lao Tzu, "Poem 64," *The Way of Life,* p. 117.
20. Kosnik et al., *Human Sexuality,* pp. 92–95.
21. St. John of the Cross, *Living Flame of Love,* p. 82.
22. St. John of the Cross, *Ascent of Mount Carmel,* p. 145.
23. *Ibid.,* p. 149.
24. Viktor Frankl, *The Doctor and the Soul* (New York: Alfred A. Knopf, 1955), p. 112.
25. Teilhard de Chardin, "L' Evolution de la Chasteté," quoted in Claude Cuénot, *Teilhard de Chardin* (Baltimore: Helicon Press, 1965), pp. 28–29.

8. EROTIC INTIMACY

1. *The Gospel According to Thomas,* trans. Puech et al., (New York: Harper & Row, 1959), pp. 17–19.
2. For a detailed explanation of the relationship between sex and religion in Taoism and Tantric Buddhism, refer to Alan Watts, *Nature, Man and Woman,* pp. 190–201. For more insight into the male and female temple prostitutes of ancient Israel, refer to Anthony Kosnik et al. *Human Sexuality,* pp. 9, 190.
3. Lao Tzu, "Poem 6," *The Way of Life,* p. 58.
4. *Ibid.,* "Poem 78," p. 131.
5. *Ibid.,* "Poem 76," p. 129.
6. Juliana of Norwich, *The Revelations of Divine Love,* trans. James Walsh (St. Meinrad, Ind.: Abbey Press, 1974), pp. 157, 161.
7. *Ibid.,* pp. 158, 168.
8. See Dante Alighieri, *The Divine Comedy, Paradise,* canto XXVIII, line 2; canto XVIII, line 4; canto X, line 93.
9. C. S. Lewis, *The Great Divorce* (New York: Macmillan, 1946), p. 108.
10. Thomas Norton, *Ordinal of Alchemy,* quoted in A. E. Waite, *The Hermetic Museum* vol. 2, art. 1 (London, 1893), p. 12.
11. Refer to St. Ambrose *De Institutione Virgines* (c. 17 Migne, PL 16), p. 442.
12. Lewis, *The Great Divorce,* p. 96.
13. Watts, *Nature, Man and Woman,* p. 168.
14. Anthony Kosnik et al., *Human Sexuality,* p. 101.
15. Dante, *Paradise,* canto X, lines 55–61.
16. *Ibid.,* canto XXX, lines 85–90.
17. See Donald Goergen, *The Sexual Celibate* (New York: Seabury, 1974), pp. 126–31.
18. Sherwin Bailey Derrick, *Sexual Relation in Christian Thought* (New York: Harper & Row, 1959), p. 33.
19. Watts, *Nature, Man and Woman,* pp. 170–71.
20. *Ibid.,* p. 171.
21. Doherty, *Poustinia,* p. 27.

9. BEYOND CELIBACY

1. Nikos Kazantzakis, *The Last Temptation of Christ* (Oxford: Bruno Cassier, 1961), p. 248.
2. *Ibid.,* p. 256.
3. William Butler Yeats, *Selected Poems,* ed. M. L. Rosenthal (New York: Macmillan, 1962), p. xx.
4. Carl Gustav Jung, *Man and His Symbols* (New York: Dell, 1964), p. 219.
5. St. Teresa of Avila, *Interior Castle,* p. 122.
6. Sigmund Freud, "Analysis of a Case of Hysteria," *Collected Papers,* vol. 3 (New York: Basic Books, 1959), pp. 131–32.
7. Kazantzakis, *The Last Temptation,* pp. 266–67.
8. Underhill, *Mysticism,* p. 210.
9. Kazantzakis, *Last Temptation,* p. 252.
10. May, *Love and Will,* p. 101.
11. St. John of the Cross, *Spiritual Canticle,* trans. E. Allison Peers (Garden City, N.Y.: Doubleday, Image Books, 1961), p. 55.
12. Underhill, *Mysticism,* p. 147.
13. Doherty, *Poustinia,* p. 131.

10. BELOVED CHILD

1. Al-Ghazahli, quoted in H. A. R. Gibb, *Mohammedanism: An Historical Survey* (New York: New American Library, 1953), p. 116.
2. Note the concern expressed in Luke 1:26–36 about celibacy and marriage. Mary is a virgin (v. 26), but she is betrothed (v. 27). Mary is to conceive a child (v. 32), but she knows not man (v. 35). It is not celibacy or marriage which will produce this son, but the "Holy Spirit," Mary's full openness to God's presence.
3. Rainer Maria Rilke, *Letters of Rainer Maria Rilke (1892–1926),* trans. Jane B. Greene and M. D. Norton (New York: W. W. Norton, 1969), Letter 74.
4. May, *Love and Will,* p. 149.
5. This is the last temptation of Jesus: not to die. The temptation is a refusal to desire the Beloved so much as to annihilate oneself.
6. St. John of the Cross, *Ascent of Mount Carmel,* pp. 193–94.
7. *Ibid.,* p. 182.
8. St. Teresa of Avila, *The Way of Perfection,* p. 215.